Democracy, Populism, and Neoliberalism in Ukraine

This book explores the reasons behind the unexpected rise to power of Ukraine's President Volodymyr Zelensky, a former comedian with no political background, and offers an in-depth analysis of the populist messages he delivered to the Ukrainian people via his TV show.

Taking a discourse analysis approach, the author draws on two main arguments of critical scholarship: the "populist explosion" of the recent decade came as a reaction to the inequalities and injustices of the global neoliberal order, and the success of neoliberalism can be explained by its ability to mask itself under attractive progressive covers. Developing these lines of argument, the book demonstrates not only how the "populist explosion" can lead to further neoliberalization, but also that the euphemizing effect can be achieved by mixing the virtual and the real, as in the case of Zelensky.

This first of its kind study will resonate with any scholar or upper-level student working on populism, neoliberalism, political communication, media studies, political science, European studies, Ukrainian studies, and discourse analysis.

Olga Baysha earned her PhD in Communication from the University of Colorado at Boulder. Previously, she worked as a news reporter and editor in Ukraine. Dr Baysha's research is on post-Soviet new media and social movements for democracy and justice.

Routledge Focus on Communication Studies

For more information about this series, please visit: https://www.routledge.com

Democracy, Populism, and Neoliberalism in Ukraine

On the Fringes of the Virtual and the Real

Olga Baysha

Routledge
Taylor & Francis Group

NEW YORK AND LONDON

First published 2022
by Routledge
605 Third Avenue, New York, NY 10158

and by Routledge
2 Park Square, Milton Park, Abingdon, Oxon OX14 4RN

Routledge is an imprint of the Taylor & Francis Group, an informa business

© 2022 Olga Baysha

British Library Cataloguing-in-Publication Data
A catalogue record for this book is available from the British Library

Library of Congress Cataloging-in-Publication Data
Names: Baysha, Olga, author.
Title: Democracy, populism and neoliberalism in Ukraine : on the
fringes of the virtual and the real / Olga Baysha.
Description: New York, NY : Routledge, 2022. | Series: Routledge
focus on communication studies | Includes bibliographical
references and index.
Identifiers: LCCN 2021043817 (print) | LCCN 2021043818
(ebook) | ISBN 9781032132310 (hardback) | ISBN 9781032132853
(paperback) | ISBN 9781003228493 (ebook)
Classification: LCC HN18.3 .B39 2022 (print) | LCC HN18.3
(ebook) | DDC 306.09477—dc23
LC record available at https://lccn.loc.gov/2021043817
LC ebook record available at https://lccn.loc.gov/2021043818

ISBN: 978-1-032-13231-0 (hbk)
ISBN: 978-1-032-13285-3 (pbk)
ISBN: 978-1-003-22849-3 (ebk)

DOI: 10.4324/9781003228493

Typeset in Bembo
by codeMantra

For Mykola Volodymyrovych Antokhov

Contents

Acknowledgments

I'm forever indebted to Justin Maki for his proofreading and editing help, keen insight, and ongoing support in bringing my academic publications to life. Thank you for sharing your time, effort, and professional expertise!

Introduction

This book is about Ukraine's latest round of neoliberal transformations, which started in 2019 after the comedian Volodymyr Zelensky scored a landslide victory in the presidential election with his *Servant of the People* party obtaining an absolute majority of parliamentary seats, empowering him to launch neoliberal reforms without regard to public opinion or the political opposition. The party, whose formation was announced only a year prior to Zelensky's dizzying electoral success, was named after the title of his television series *Servant of the People*, in which the future president played the role of Vasyl Petrovych Holoborodko—a fictional head of state who, after a fluke ascent to the presidency from his humble job as a history teacher, manages to transform Ukraine into a prosperous country by demolishing the oligarchic system of power and eradicating omnipresent corruption.

The argument presented in this book is that the astonishing victory of the comedian and his party, later transformed into a parliamentary machine to churn out and rubber-stamp neoliberal reforms (in a "turbo regime," as the "servants" called it), cannot be explained apart from the success of his television series, which, as many observers believe, served as Zelensky's informal election platform. Unlike his official platform, which ran only 1,601 words in length and contained few policy specifics, the 51 half-hour episodes of his show provided Ukrainians with a detailed vision of what should be done so that Ukraine could progress.

Zelensky's election promises, made on the fringes of the virtual and the real, were predominantly about Ukraine's "progress," understood as "modernization," "Westernization," "civilization," and "normalization." It is this progressive modernizing discourse that allowed Zelensky to camouflage his plans for neoliberal reforms, launched just three days after the new government came to power. Throughout the campaign, the idea of "progress" highlighted by Zelensky was never linked

DOI: 10.4324/9781003228493-1

to privatization, land sales, budget cuts, etc. Only after Zelensky had consolidated his presidential power by establishing full control over the legislative and executive branches of power did he make it clear that the "normalization" and "civilization" of Ukraine meant the privatization of land and state/public property, the deregulation of labor relations, a reduction of power for trade unions, an increase in utility tariffs, and so on.

To analyze Zelensky's "progressive" discourse that masked his plans for neoliberal experimentation, this book refers to Nancy Fraser's (2019) theory of progressive neoliberalism. Fraser posits that, in order to triumph, a neoliberal project needs "to be repackaged, given a broader appeal, and linked to other, noneconomic aspirations for emancipation" (p. 13). In other words, it needs to "euphemize itself" (Phelan, 2007), masking the omnipresent marketization of all aspects of the social under an attractive progressive cover. Fraser's focus is on new social movements that, in her view, have enabled such euphemization by lending their charisma to the neoliberal project. This book extends the scope of Fraser's argument by considering the term "progress" an empty/floating signifier, capable of being linked to different associations—not only to identity politics. As the case of Zelensky suggests, neoliberal discourse may be euphemized through linking "progress" to "modernization," "civilization," and "Westernization."

This book is written in a discourse-theoretical tradition: Analysis presented herein builds on the discourse theory of Ernesto Laclau and Chantal Mouffe (1985), which postulates that social meanings are not pre-given but emerge through articulatory practices. Using this theory, the book analyzes Zelensky's pre-election populism and traces how his show drew a solid antagonistic frontier between "the people" and "the elites," dividing Ukraine into two non-overlapping entities: "good us" ("the people") vs. "bad them" (corrupted elites). The constructed equivalential chain of bankrupt morals and primitive intellect—as was applied to the establishment—did not presuppose much possibility for meaningful communication with such people. Instead, this antagonistic presentation prescribed a swift and total shunning: lustration, imprisonment, property expropriation, and so forth. As this book shows, later, during Zelensky's real presidency, such a presentation of the parliamentary opposition gave "servants" the moral right to disregard opposing views.

In analyzing Zelensky's populism, the book also refers to Laclau's (2005) theorizing of "populism" as a political logic—a way of constituting the people—that is not identifiable with a specific ideological orientation or social base. This outlook, as De Cleen and colleagues

(2018) suggest, goes against treating populism "as a symptomatic effect of socio-economic and socio-cultural changes... [that]... create grievances, discontent and crises that populist political actors capitalize on" (p. 651). In line with De Cleen and his colleagues, this book assumes that discontentment among the people does not automatically transform into populist politics—the success of the latter cannot be reduced to an objective outcome of particular socio-economic developments. However, the book also recognizes that mass dissatisfaction with this or that socio-economic development may inform a populist project by providing its leaders with an opportunity to articulate mass discontentment as anti-elitist sentiment among the people.

For this reason, analysis in the book is attentive to the observations of numerous critical scholars who claim that the populist explosion (Judis, 2016) witnessed over the last two decades has resulted from people's indignation about the injustices of the neoliberal order (e.g., Butler, 2016; Fraser, 2019; Harvey, 2018; Žižek, 2018). In line with these critical scholars, the book argues that the success of Zelensky's populist project also drew on people's dissatisfaction with the neoliberal order; however, it focuses primarily on how people's dissatisfaction has been articulated in Zelensky's interviews, speeches, and the television show—how "the people" and "the elites" have been created discursively, and what political outcomes these discursive constructions implied.

Apart from treating populism as a concept possessing its own logic (the discursive/political construction of "the people"), this book also takes it as an empty signifier that acquires its meaning through linkage to other elements of the discursive-material field (Carpentier, 2017). This shift from understanding populism as a concept to taking it as an empty signifier enables the discerning of populism's strategic dimension through tracing how a populist discourse can be employed for a strategic purpose—for example, for the acquisition of power then used for reactionary politics. As Aurelien Mondon and Aaron Winter (2020) put it,

> the resurgence of racism, populism and the far right is not the result of popular demands, as we are often told, but instead the logical conclusion of the more or less conscious manipulation of the concept of 'the people' to push reactionary ideas in the service of power.
>
> (p. 5)

Manipulating the concept of "the people" for strategic purposes is central to the case of Zelensky. As this book suggests, it was Zelensky's pre-election populism that allowed him to win the 2019 presidential election and create a parliamentary machine for adopting neoliberal legislation without regard for public opinion, which was characterized by massive opposition to the reforms.

With respect to "neoliberalism," this book similarly considers it as an empty signifier: There are assumed to be multiple versions of it, and each of these versions is "a moving matrix of articulations" (Peck & Theodore, 2019, p. 246). In other words, it is assumed that neoliberalism cannot be reduced to a singular policy package applicable to all situations—the policy combinations vary, as do their meanings created through discursive-material assemblages. Nor can it be reduced to the writings of Friedrich Hayek, Milton Friedman, and other founding neoliberal intellectuals as "actually existing neoliberalisms" deviate significantly from what these founding fathers envisaged (Brown, 2019).

While admitting that any neoliberal project has its local peculiarities and conjunctural specificities, this book is nonetheless in line with those critical scholars who believe the term "neoliberalism," despite all its vagueness, is still analytically useful (e.g., Davies, 2017; Slobodian, 2020; Wilson, 2018). The stance taken on this issue supports Wendy Brown's (2018) argument that we do not abandon the terms "capitalism," "socialism," or "liberalism" just because they may have different meanings in different contexts. Why should we abandon the term "neoliberalism," even if it cannot represent the full complexity of each separate case? "Neoliberalism is semiotically loose," Brown (2018) argues, "but designates something very specific. It represents a distinctive kind of valorization and liberation of capital. It makes economics the model of everything [including the] economization of democracy" (p. 3).

More specifically, with respect to the post-Soviet reforming of Ukraine, the discussion of "neoliberalism" presented in this book focuses predominantly on the policy package of privatization, deregulation, and liberalization—part of what IMF analysts acknowledge to be essential parts of many neoliberal projects (Ostry et al., 2016). While discussing Zelensky's neoliberal reforms, the book also builds on Quinn Slobodian's (2020) insight about neoliberalism's tendency to abolish the "excesses" of democracy and national sovereignty through redesigning the state and creating a global institutional regime of safeguarding the free market.

As this book argues, it appears as if Zelensky, in harmony with classic neoliberal thinking that spurns the inclusive and comprehensive political processes on which robust democracy rests, has been trying to defend his neoliberal project from democratic pressures, using his party machine and unconstitutional methods of consolidating presidential power to advance his goals. Zelensky's project, in terms of its effort to guard itself from "democratic excesses," is far from unique—"the disenchantment of politics by economics" (Davies, 2017, p. xx) is a general feature of neoliberalism. However, Zelensky's contribution to the general trend includes a major innovation: The condition of possibility for Zelensky's neoliberal project was the creation of a zone of exception where the virtual and the real were not mutually exclusive, but instead blurred into one another.

To analyze this aspect of Zelensky's story, the book employs Nico Carpentier's model of the Discursive-Material Knot (2017), which is expanded by incorporating the materiality of the digital. It also refers to Jean Baudrillard's (2005) theory of an "integral universe" in which "reality is disappearing at the hands of the cinema and the cinema is disappearing at the hands of reality" (p. 125), and where the very principle of opposition is destroyed. It is argued that the dismantling of the political—a logical outcome of the dismantling of the principle of opposition—is one of the main features of Zelensky's neoliberal authoritarianism that has been forged on the fringes of the virtual and the real.

The analysis presented in this book is based on all 51 episodes in the three-season run of Zelensky's series *Servant of the People*, the election platforms of Zelensky and his party, and Zelensky's speeches, interviews, press conferences, and video blogs. All of Zelensky's public appearances and remarks (video and in print) have been monitored daily since December 31, 2018, when, on the eve of the new year, he announced his decision to run for president. Overall, 357 discursive constructions have been analyzed. For the analysis of the rhetoric employed by Zelensky and his allies to push forward their land reform, video records of two parliamentary sessions were used: one from November 13, 2019, when the new land code was passed in the first reading, and the other from March 31, 2020, when it was adopted in the second reading.

References

Baudrillard, J. (2005). *The intelligence of evil.* New York: Berg.

Brown, W. (2018, January 18). Who is not a neoliberal today? *Tocqueville 21.* Retrieved from www.tocqueville21.com/interviews/wendy-brown-not-neoliberal-today

Brown, W. (2019). *In the ruins of neoliberalism.* New York: Columbia University Press.

Butler, J. (2016, October 28). Trump is emancipating unbridled hatred. *Zeit Online.* Retrieved from https://www.zeit.de/kultur/2016-10/judith-butler-donald-trump-populism-interview

Carpentier, N. (2017). *The discursive-material knot: Cyprus in conflict and community media participation.* New York: Peter Lang.

Davies, W. (2017). *The limits of neoliberalism: Authority, sovereignty and the logic of competition.* London: Sage.

De Cleen, B., Glynos, J., & Mondon, A. (2018). Critical research on populism: Nine rules of engagement. *Organization, 25*(5), 649–661.

Fraser, N. (2019). *The old is dying and the new cannot be born: From progressive neoliberalism to Trump and beyond.* New York: Verso.

Harvey, D. (2018). Universal alienation. *TripleC, 16*(2), 424–439. doi: 10.31269/triplec.v16i2.1026

Judis, J. (2016). *The populist explosion: How the great recession transformed American and European politics.* New York: Columbia Global Reports.

Laclau, E., & Mouffe, C. (1985). *Hegemony and socialist strategy: Towards a radical democratic politics.* London: Verso.

Laclau, E. (2005). *On populist reason.* New York: Verso.

Mondon, A., & Winter, A. (2020). *Reactionary democracy: How racism and the populist far right became mainstream.* New York: Verso Books.

Ostry, J. D., Loungani, P., & Furceri, D. (2016, May 31). Neoliberalism: Oversold? Instead of delivering growth, some neoliberal policies have increased inequality, in turn jeopardizing durable expansion. *Finance & Development, 53*(002), 38–41.

Peck, J., & Theodore, N. (2019). Still neoliberalism? *South Atlantic Quarterly, 118*(2), 245–265. doi: 10.1215/00382876-7381122

Phelan, S. (2007). The discourses of neoliberal hegemony: The case of the Irish Republic. *Critical Discourse Studies, 4*(1), 29–48. doi: 10.1080/17405900601149459

Slobodian, Q. (2020). *Globalists: The end of empire and the birth of neoliberalism.* Cambridge, MA: Harvard University Press.

Wilson, J. A. (2018). *Neoliberalism.* New York: Routledge.

Žižek, S. (2018). The prospects of radical change today. *TripleC, 16*(2), 476–489. doi: 10.31269/triplec.v16i2.1023

1 The Populist Explosion as a Reaction to the Neoliberal Order

The Return of the Repressed

Many critical thinkers believe that the rise of contemporary populism—"the populist explosion," as John Judis (2016) dubbed it—has come about as a reaction to the inequalities and injustices of the TINA ("There Is No Alternative") neoliberal order by those whom this order has neglected, betrayed, and impoverished. According to Chantal Mouffe (2016), "the 'post-political' situation has created a favourable terrain for populist parties that claim to represent all who feel unheard and ignored in the existing representative system." In Judith Butler's (2016) view, populists mobilize "more and more people who are abandoned and dispossessed… without discriminating between right and left." "Liberal political agendas, neoliberal economic agendas, and cosmopolitan cultural agendas generated a growing experience of abandonment, betrayal, and ultimately rage on the part of the new dispossessed," Wendy Brown (2019, p. 3) observes, while David Harvey (2018, p. 424) notes that "[w]idespread alienation has resulted in Occupy movements as well as right-wing populism and bigoted nationalist and racist movements." Pierre-André Taguieff (2016) asserts that "[t]he rejection of destructive globalization and illegitimate elites propels the loss of left-right divisions [and] unites former opponents [who] overlap, intertwine, merge in some cases." Advances by populist parties in Italy's 2018 elections and Germany's coalition-building the same year "merely confirm the disappearance of the modest Social-Democratic Left and the rise of the new populism as the only (fake) alternative to global capitalism," Slavoj Žižek (2018, p. 486) argues. "In every case, voters are saying 'No!' to the lethal combination of austerity, free trade, predatory debt and precarious, ill-paid work that characterizes present-day financialized capitalism," Nancy Fraser maintains (2017, p. 40). A complete list of similar claims would be extensive.

DOI: 10.4324/9781003228493-2

"As long as global inequality, uncertainty and fear will keep growing," Yannis Stavrakakis (2017) suggests, "the demands of the impoverished, neglected and forgotten middle and lower classes will intensify" (p. 531). Since these demands are usually presented in populist terms through the construction of antagonistic frontiers between "the people" and "the elites," it may be expected, Stavrakakis claims, that the struggles of "the impoverished, neglected, and forgotten" will be framed as "populist." In line with Stavrakakis's (2017) observation that populism always "disrupts a supposed 'normal' course of events and can only be seen as a signal of failure" (p. 524), all the latest populist developments—from the left-wing populism in Greece, Spain, or Italy to the right-wing populism in France, Austria, or Finland—look "as if masses of people throughout the world had stopped believing in the reigning common sense that has underpinned political domination for the last several decades," as Fraser (2019, p. 8) puts it.

In this sense, the populist success of Volodymyr Zelensky, which this book analyzes, is not an exception. As in the cases discussed by the authors cited above, the popular discontent that brought Zelensky to power had also been informed by people's indignation regarding the injustices and inequalities of the neoliberal order. In Ukraine, the advent of this order in the 1990s manifested itself in the scrapping of the Soviet welfare system, the privatization of once collective/state property, and the formation of the oligarchic class—the *nouveau riches* who made their fortunes from people's impoverishment. Criticism of the oligarchic system of power, which was formed during the first decade of Ukraine's independence, was a leitmotif of Zelensky's presidential campaign. Accordingly, the story of Zelensky's success should be traced back as far as Gorbachev's *perestroika*, when the ideological foundations of the future neoliberalization were put in place. It was during *perestroika* that the ideology of universal progress became hegemonic, and it was this ideology that sanctioned all further neoliberal reforms, including Zelensky's.

According to this "progressive" vision, which came to be taken as normal during Gorbachev's rule, the West (always imagined in universal terms, without internal contradictions) appeared as a model of social justice and the historical avant-garde leading humanity toward a "normality" imagined in singular terms. This new sensibility allowed the citizens of the former Soviet states, including Ukraine, first to believe that neoliberalization (imagined as Westernization and normalization) would make their states democratic and prosperous; and later, that getting rid of oligarchs and corruption would allow them to achieve a perfect Western-like condition with social justice and equality for all (more on this in the next section).

To understand the dizzying political success of Zelensky, a comedian who ridiculed the political establishment but had no political experience of his own, it is also necessary to get an idea of what happened in Ukraine in the aftermath of the Euromaidan revolution of 2013–2014—the "revolution of dignity against Yanukovych's[1] corrupted regime," as the revolutionary narrative dubbed it. During the revolution, which was also conditioned by the contradictions of the neoliberal order, Ukraine was split into two irreconcilable parts holding diametrically opposed views on both the revolution and its politico-economic consequences. The reconciliation of Ukraine—its symbolic reunification—was the premise on which Zelensky's populism depended. I will discuss this in more detail after presenting the legacy of *perestroika*, which laid the foundation for all further neoliberal experiments.

The Legacy of *Perestroika*

Gorbachev started *perestroika* in the mid-1980s, when the necessity of change seemed obvious for many people living in the USSR. The inflexibility of centralized decision-making had resulted in imbalances across the whole economic system and an inability to satisfy people's needs, leading to omnipresent shortages of consumer goods. A giant shadow economy was formed, involving the highest state officials (party *nomenklatura*). While receiving shadow rents in close collaboration with "red directors" (managers of huge industrial enterprises) and "teneviki" (underground economic players), such officials blocked any possibility of positive change, although later they were the ones who benefited most from the neoliberal reforms that followed *perestroika* (on this aspect of *perestroika* see, for example, Castells, 2010).

Suffering from bureaucratic surveillance over cultural life and scientific research, Soviet intellectuals were among the first to support Gorbachev's *glasnost*—the policy of a gradual reduction of censorship—an important part of *perestroika* aimed at the democratization of the public sphere. In the beginning, Gorbachev's reform was also widely greeted by Soviet working people who supported the idea of "updating socialism," one of Gorbachev's initial promises (Gorbachev, 1986). He hoped to reboot the Soviet project by overcoming the resistance of *nomenklatura*, the military-industrial complex, and the bosses of the shadow economy through the mobilization of popular support.

But Gorbachev's policy of *glasnost*, designed to bolster his modernizing socialist project, brought unexpected consequences. Instead of discussing how the socialist project could be improved, new media, liberated from party control, formed a nourishing milieu for new intellectual elites who favored neoliberal—not socialist—reformation (Turpin, 1995). It was these Soviet liberals who introduced their mass Soviet audiences to the neoliberal mythology of *laissez-faire* economics in which magic, self-regulating markets are capable of granting equality, freedom, justice, and happiness for all (Bockman, 2011; Krausz, 2007; Shlapentokh, 1993). The new media played a crucial role in the spread of the ideology of neoliberalism that "installs in its subjects a belief in markets—anything else fails, is inefficient, can't be funded, won't last, can't compete in a global arena" (Dean, 2009, p. 48). Very quickly, this ideology was normalized to the point of becoming common sense.

Importantly, during *perestroika*, Gorbachev also experienced an ideological shift, as is evident from his speeches of the 1990s. "Spiritual progress can be successfully implemented today only in the channel of the common development of civilization," he argued in 1991 (Gorbachev in Brown, 2007, p. 236). This statement clearly testifies that by this time Gorbachev had come to accept the ideology of universal progress, with the belief in a common developmental route and common destiny for all humankind. The implication of such a belief was that the West, as leader of the world community, was "destined to move ahead of the huge advancing column" while all others followed, as Charles Taylor sarcastically put it (1992, p. 424).

For Richard Sakwa (2005), it is obvious that by the 1990s Gorbachev was "no longer thinking in Leninist terms and had accepted the justice of Eduard Bernstein's revisionist arguments" (p. 258). However, what looks obvious today was not necessarily so back in the 1990s. The main problem, which nourishes both nostalgia for the USSR (Boele et al., 2019) and the populist mood in post-Soviet states today, is that the fundamental shift in the views of *perestroika* ideologists went unrecognized by many citizens of the Soviet state until they had already been delivered into the "heaven" of neoliberal civilizational advance. In public discourse by *perestroika* ideologists, the transformation was not about capitalization and marketization, but about "progress," "civilization," "modernization," "democratization," "liberalization," and so forth. In other words, to use Pierre Bourdieu's (1998) concept—more on this in Chapter 2—their neoliberal promise was euphemized, being masked by attractive modernizing and civilizing covers.

According to Vladimir Shlapentokh, "pure" (or "transparent," to put it in Sean Phelan's [2007] terms) market ideas—not covered with a civilizational fig leaf—started to be openly propagated only after 1991, when, following the "parade of state sovereignties," it became clear that reviving the Soviet socialist project was no longer a realistic expectation. Now, when discursive attempts to marry socialism and capitalism could finally be abandoned, the pure neoliberal discourse of privatization displaced the narrative of "self-management" of collective property by working collectives—an invention of Abel Gezevich Aganbegyan (1988), Gorbachev's chief economic advisor. At the beginning of *perestroika*, self-management—a very popular idea among Soviet workers—was imagined as a means of destroying the Soviet bureaucratic machine and forcing economic progress.

To be sure, the masking of neoliberal transformations with discourse of "updating socialism," "democratization," "civilization," etc., was not always a conscious manipulation. The policies of *perestroika* were not an object of theoretical analysis; they appeared as a result of the practical necessity of implementing economic reforms to improve the lives of the Soviet people. Without the proper theoretical awareness, Gorbachev and those working closely with him turned out to be unable to foresee the consequences of their actions, and as a result, "*perestroika* was fast becoming the means of an antisocialist 'change of system'" (Krausz, 2007, p. 12). This happened because the Soviet leadership "proved to be remarkably naive in evaluating the political implications of this process (of major structural transformations)" and because their policies were "based on serious misreading of economic realities" (Buck-Morss, 2000, p. 265).

Partly because of that theoretical naivety and partly because of strategic manipulations aimed at mollifying public opinion unfavorable to market reforms—when the phrase "civil property" was used instead of "private property" (Krausz, 2007) and "collectivization" instead of "privatization" (Shlapentokh, 1993)—important preconditions were set up for the emergence of new elites who veiled their interest in the transition to a market economy with rhetoric of civilizational progress linked to modernization, democratization, and so on. Moreover, the simplification of the historical narrative and its presentation as a mythical fight between democratic/progressive/civilizational good and non-democratic/retrograde/barbarian evil had far-reaching consequences. Eventually, it transformed protesters against market reforms—those who may rightfully have been termed enemies of neoliberalism—into enemies of democracy and progress. Suffice it to mention Boris Yeltsin's order for tanks to attack the Russian parliament building and shell it into ruins rather than permit legislators to check the unregulated marketization of Russia. In official discourse, this was presented as "democratization" (Snyder, 2018, p. 44).

Albeit exceptional in terms of its physical violence, Yeltsin's example is rather typical in its equation of neoliberalization with democratization, modernization, and progress. Symbolic violence against millions of working people whose resistance to neoliberalization was taken as an unwillingness to be civilized and democratized has been omnipresent (Baysha, 2014). In the eyes of the propagandists for "civilization" and "democratization" (equated to neoliberalism), the unwillingness of working people to appropriate capitalist modernity looked like ignorance, backwardness, stupidity, and laziness. The collectivism of Soviet culture was imagined as a soil in which "the most dreadful and ugly things in history have grown" [вырастало все самое страшное и уродливое в нашей истории] (Mitrokhin, 1990), something that needed to be eradicated no matter what, as *perestroika* activists believed. "The dragon must be killed," wrote Valeria Novodvorskaya, the leader of the Democratic Union, invoking the title of one of the most popular *perestroika*-era movies, *To Kill the Dragon*:

> Bolshevism is the prolongation of the autocratic history of Russia. Faithful. Servile. Collectivist. In order to transform to democracy, we need to overcome not only Soviet history but Russian history as well. We need to change our consciousness.... To become different and to scramble out of our skins.... We need to kill dragons in ourselves.

> [Большевизм—это продолжение автократической истории России. Верноподданической. Холопской. Коллективистской. Поэтому нам для перехода к демократии... нам придется изменить свое сознание.... Стать другими и вылезти из своей шкуры.... Уничтожить драконов в себе].
> (Novodvorskaya, 1990, p. 3)

The consequences of this "dragon hunt" are well known. Through the unregulated and uncontrolled mass privatization of the 1990s, state enterprises "were sold for ridiculous prices for whoever had the money and the power to control the transaction" (Castells, 2010, p. 193). The "whoever" in this case consisted of party *nomenklatura*, red directors, and other members of the Soviet establishment who accumulated wealth during the era of Brezhnev's stagnation by profiting from systemic shortages and during *perestroika* by depositing state funds into personal bank accounts abroad. Most of Ukraine's oligarchs, including "the chocolate king" Petro Poroshenko—Zelensky's rival in the 2019 presidential election—were among those individuals who had amassed fortunes through the mass impoverishment of working people during the first decade of post-Soviet neoliberal reforms, when the newly independent states were being picked clean by those who had privileged access to former state resources.

For Ukraine, the consequences of these "reforms" were devastating: The country was pushed into one of the deepest recessions experienced by any of the transition economies not affected by war (Usher, 1998):

> GDP fell by 57 per cent between 1989 and 1998. Inflation went from 200 per cent in 1991 to hyperinflation following the removal of price controls on demand of the IMF and reached 2,730 per cent in 1992, and 10,155 per cent in 1993...
>
> After decades of full employment under Soviet rule, first 350,000 registered in 1997 and 1.2 million officially, up to 7 million unofficially were without jobs.
>
> (Yurchenko, 2018, p. 86)

With people's savings "wiped out and their salaries not keeping up with prices, three quarters of Ukrainians lived below the poverty level" (Yekelchuk, 2015, p. 77).

Mass poverty was strongly associated with the "mortality crisis" and a "suicide epidemic explained by the macroeconomic instability" (Brainerd, 2001, p. 1007). In Ukraine, "between 1989 and 1994 mortality rates rose by 25% and life expectancy dropped by 3 years" (Dyczok, 2000, pp. 90–91). In 2009, the *Lancet,* a British medical journal, published an article arguing that the clear culprit for the "drop, of fully five years in male life expectancy between 1991 and 1994" was the "shock therapy" of market reforms. It argued that the "advocates of freemarket economics … ignored the human costs of the policies they were promoting. These included unemployment and human misery, leading to early death. In effect, mass privatisation was mass murder" (Economist, 2009). No wonder the many working people of the former Soviet Ukraine have no sympathy either for oligarchs—the newly rich who made fortunes through stealing people's collective property—or for the discourses of "civilization," "modernization," and "democratization" that covered these crimes.

Popular resentment against oligarchy—the product of Ukraine's neoliberalization of the 1990s—became an important factor in Zelensky's electoral victory in 2019 over Poroshenko, the owner of a "chocolate empire" consisting of several confectioneries privatized during the "non-payment crisis" of the 1990s, when state enterprises were unable to pay their debts (Sigal, 2014). What is no less important for understanding Zelensky's victory over the "chocolate king" is that the latter's ascent to become the fifth president of Ukraine (2014–2019) had occurred on the wave of the Euromaidan revolution. As stated earlier, the consequences of the Euromaidan, which split the country into two irreconcilable parts, was another crucial factor that paved the way for Zelensky to reach the heights of political power. The prospect of reconciliation—Ukraine's symbolic reunification—was the backbone of Zelensky's inclusionary populism.

The Euromaidan and Its "Deplorables"

Euromaidan (also called Maidan) protests started in Kyiv in late November 2013, when a group of young protesters—predominantly students, in the beginning—expressed their discontent regarding the refusal of President Yanukovych to sign an Association Agreement (AA) with the European Union. This agreement was an extension of the European Neighborhood Policy (ENP) project launched by the EU in 2004 with an idea of creating a comfort zone around the Union—a "ring of friends" that would be aligned with the West though without necessarily becoming EU members. The dominant view shared among the protesters was that Yanukovych's decision not to sign the agreement with the EU resulted from Russia's attempts to force Ukraine to join the Eurasian Economic Union (EEU)—a Russia-led geopolitical enterprise. In the eyes of Euromaidan protesters, these two projects were signified with diametrically opposite meanings. The AA was seen predominantly in terms of democratization, modernization, and civilization—it was imagined as a means of bringing Ukraine up to European standards of government by fighting against oligarchs and corruption while seeking improvements in areas such as the supremacy of law, equality for all, and government transparency (Áslund, 2015; Wilson, 2014; Yekelchuk, 2015). In contrast, the EEU was associated with civilizational regression to Soviet statism and Asian despotism (Baysha, 2015).

It is here that the positions of Euromaidan liberals and nationalists converged: The latter actively supported the Euromaidan not because of democratization, but due to its clear anti–Russia stance. From the first days of the protests, radical nationalists were the most active Maidan fighters (Ishchenko, 2020). As Sakwa (2015) put it, "ultimately, the profound civic impetus for dignity and good governance at the heart of the Maidan revolution was hijacked by the radicals" (p. 131). The unity between liberals associating the Euromaidan with progress, modernization, human rights, etc., and radicals co-opting the movement for their nationalistic agenda was an important prerequisite for the transformation of the civic protest into an armed struggle resulting in an unconstitutional overturning of power. The decisive role of radicals in the revolution also became a crucial factor in the formation of a mass anti-Maidan movement in the east of Ukraine against the "coup d'etat," as the hegemonic anti-Maidan discourse dubbed the change of power in Kyiv (Sakwa, 2015).

With respect to the topic of this book, it is important to recognize that although "the association agreement has always been seen in highly politicized and symbolic terms as a 'civilizational choice' in which Ukraine would be able to leave behind its dark, eastern past and march forward into the safety and comfort of the European Union," as Mark Adomanis (2014) correctly points out,

> In reality the association agreement has nothing to do with culture or history and is much more basic: a highly technocratic bit of economic liberalization. There is no "European" way to end gas subsidies, and no "civilized" way to cut pensions. These steps are either taken or they are avoided. Since economic liberalization is not very popular in Ukraine, since Ukrainians continue to express extremely left-wing economic views, the struggle to implement free trade is likely to be long and nasty.

Indeed, in looking at the Joint Declaration of the Eastern Partnership Summit in Vilnius where Yanukovych had a chance to sign the AA, it is easy to see how the discourse of democratization legitimized and masked the neoliberal agenda of the EU's policy toward Ukraine by using the word "democracy" instead of "market," and presenting neoliberalization as "democratization" (Baysha, 2020a). The true meaning of "democratization" proposed by the Declaration becomes evident when one looks at Paragraph 7, which refers to "the unprecedented public support for Ukraine's political association and economic integration with the EU" (Declaration, 2013, p. 3). The reality was radically different: Opinion polls conducted in Ukraine on the eve of the Vilnius Summit showed that less than half of Ukraine's population (39%) supported the idea of European association at that point in time (KIIS, 2013). The most strident opposition to the AA was in Donbas—a highly industrial region whose inhabitants suffered most from the country's post-Soviet neoliberal reforms (Mykhnenko, 2003; Siegelbaum, 1997; Swain, 2006).

Because of this, in the hegemonic discourse of the Maidan that equated the revolution with democratization and progress, Donbas residents opposing European integration and the change of Ukrainian power committed in its name were given the status of "sovki" (the plural form of "sovok" [совки/совок]—a derogatory term to denote someone with a "Soviet mentality"), "slaves," "underdeveloped barbarians," "modernization's losers," and the like (Baysha, 2015). Some Maidan activists believed that Donbas "should be flattened and covered with cement" because its residents were "different from the rest of Ukraine" and deemed to be "pro-Soviet" (Zhuravlev & Ishchenko, 2020, p. 226).

The dominant tendency among both Maidan leaders and activists was to present Ukrainians who had not supported the revolution as the country's radical outside: "non-citizens" who did not deserve to be part of the community of "Ukrainian people," as equated with the community of Maidan supporters. Here is a very typical example of such a presentation of anti-Maidan "others":

> I am not talking about the split along the East-West…. I am talking about a more bitter and more essential phenomenon that is typical for all regions—the distinction between the people and the population, between citizens and slaves.

> [Я не про поділ по лінії Схід-Захід… [Я] Про гіркіше й набагато суттєвіше, характерне для всіх регіонів—про співвідношення народ-населення, або громадяни-раби].
>
> (Hrytsenko, 2013)

This is how Anatoliy Hrytsenko, a former Minister of Defense (2005–2007) and an incumbent People's Deputy of Ukraine, saw those opposing the Euromaidan revolution. Such a view has been typical among Euromaidan activists.

The Euromaidan movement was composed of different groups of protesters who were there to push different agendas—Euro-romantics seeking Westernization, liberals struggling against abuses of power, nationalist radicals pursuing strictly anti-Russia goals, and so forth. However, this diversity remained invisible in the speeches of Maidan leaders (Baysha, 2020c). In their representation of the movement, the empty signifier "Maidan" came to denote the impossible unity of all the people of Ukraine—"the nation of free people" [нація вільних людей], as Yulia Tymoshenko (2014), a well-known Ukrainian politician, put it.[2] Not a single leader of the Euromaidan problematized this constructed equivalence between "the people of Ukraine" and "the people of the Maidan"; in all their representations, the latter and the former were wholly the same. The basic problem with this representation was that, as mentioned earlier, half of Ukraine's population did not support the movement.

Accordingly, the internal split within Ukraine, which has deep historical roots (Plokhy, 2008), only intensified after the victory of the revolution. Proof of this can be found in UN reports. "With the passage of time," one of them claimed, "divisions in Ukrainian society resulting from the conflict will continue to deepen and take root" (UN OHCHR, 2017, p. 40). Even today, seven years after the Maidan, it is still normal for citizens of Ukraine on opposite sides of the revolution to hurl insults at each other, including specific neologisms that came to life during the Maidan; for example, "vatniki" [ватники] is used by Maidan supporters to cast opponents as "Russian coats" stuffed with cotton instead of brains, while anti-Maidan stalwarts call its proponents "pan-heads" [кастрюлеголовые] empty of intelligence or reason (Baysha, 2020b). Through these and similar neologisms, two impossible unities were discursively formed as each side characterized the other as mentally sick, stupid, infantile, and brainwashed. The "vatnik" condition of Maidan opponents (predominantly Russian-speakers living in southeastern regions) referred to their assumed "backwardness," while the "pan-head" condition of Maidan supporters (predominantly Ukrainian-speakers living in northwestern regions) referred to "brainlessness" and an inability to foresee the consequences of their uprising: namely, the annexation of Crimea, the war in Donbas, a dramatic increase in utility costs, and a similarly dramatic deterioration of living conditions after the Maidan (Knoblock, 2020).

It is against this backdrop that the presidential election of 2019, which made Zelensky the sixth president of Ukraine, took place. As will be shown in Chapters 3 and 4, the symbolic stitching up of the torn Ukraine that Zelensky performed on his show by juxtaposing "the Ukrainian people" against its radical outside—oligarchs and corrupted politicians—came to be an important factor in his populist success.

Notes

1 Victor Yanukovych was the fourth president of Ukraine (2010–2014). His system of power was so corrupt that Transparency International ranked Ukraine 144 out of 177 countries on its Corruption Perceptions Index (Åslund, 2014).
2 Yulia Tymoshenko is the leader of the All-Ukrainian Union "Fatherland" political party. She served as the prime minister of Ukraine in 2005 and from 2007 to 2010.

References

Adomanis, M. (2014, June 27). Ukraine, Russia, and the European Union. *Forbes*. Retrieved from http://www.forbes.com/sites/markadomanis/2014/06/27/Ukraine-russia-and-the-european-union-the-end-of-the-beginning/

Aganbegyan, A. G. (1988). *The challenge: Economics of perestroika*. London: Hutchinson Education.

Áslund, A. (2014). Oligarchs, corruption, and European Integration. *Journal of Democracy, 25*(3), 64–73. doi: 10.1353/jod.2014.0055

Áslund, A. (2015). *Ukraine: What went wrong and how to fix it.* Washington, DC: Peterson Institute for International Economics.

Baysha, O. (2014). *The mythologies of capitalism and the end of the Soviet project.* Lanham, MD: Lexington.

Baysha, O. (2015). Ukrainian Euromaidan: The exclusion of otherness in the name of progress. *European Journal of Cultural Studies, 18*(1), 3–18. doi: 10.1177/1367549414557806

Baysha, O. (2020a). Deconstructing the coloniality of the West-centric democratic imaginary. *Cadernos de Linguagem e Sociedade, 21*(1), 21–41. doi: 10.26512/les.v21i1.30389

Baysha, O. (2020b). The antagonistic discourses of the Euromaidan: Koloradi, Sovki, and Vatniki vs. Jumpers, Maidowns, and Panheads. In N. Knoblock (Ed.), *Language of conflict: Discourses of the Ukrainian crisis* (pp. 101–117). London: Bloomsbury Academic.

Baysha, O. (2020c). The impossible totality of Ukraine's "people": On the populist discourse of the Ukrainian maidan. In M. Kranert (Ed.), *Discursive approaches to populism across disciplines* (pp. 63–90). Switzerland: Springer Nature.

Bockman, J. (2011). *Markets in the name of socialism.* Stanford, CA: Stanford University Press.

Boele, O., Noordenbos, B., & Robbe, K. (2019). *Post-Soviet Nostalgia: Confronting the empire's legacies.* New York: Routledge.

Bourdieu, P. (1998). *Acts of resistance: Against the new myths of our times.* Cambridge, MA: Polity Press.

Brainerd, E. (2001). Economic reform and mortality in the former Soviet Union: A study of the suicide epidemic in the 1990s. *European Economic Review, 45*(4), 1007–1019. doi: 10.1016/S0014-2921(01)00108-8

Brown, A. (2007). Gorbachev, Lenin, and the break with Leninism in Russia. *Demokratizatsiya. The Journal of Post-Soviet Democratization, 15*(2), 230–244. doi: 10.17976/jpps/2007.06.08

Brown, W. (2019). *In the ruins of neoliberalism.* New York: Columbia University Press.

Buck-Morss, S. (2000). *Dreamworld and catastrophe: The passing of mass utopia in East and West.* Cambridge, MA: MIT Press.

Butler, J. (2016, October 28). Trump is emancipating unbridled hatred. *Zeit Online.* Retrieved from https://www.zeit.de/kultur/2016-10/judith-butler-donald-trump-populism-interview

Castells, M. (2010). *End of millennium.* Oxford, MA: Blackwell.

Dean, J. (2009). *Democracy and other neoliberal fantasies.* Durham, NC & London: Duke University Press.

Declaration. (2013, May 29). Joint declaration of the Eastern partnership summit. *Council of the European Union.* Retrieved from https://www.consilium.europa.eu/media/31799/2013_eap-11-28-joint-declaration.pdf. Accessed May 29, 2020.

Dyczok, M. (2000). *Ukraine: Movement without change, change without movement.* Amsterdam: Overseas Publishers Association.

Economist. (2009, January 22). Mass murder and the market. Retrieved from http://www.economist.com/node/12972677

Fraser, N. (2017). Progressive neoliberalism versus reactionary populism: A Hobson's choice. In H. Geiselberger (Ed.), *The great regression* (pp. 40–49). Cambridge: Polity Press.

Fraser, N. (2019). *The old is dying and the new cannot be born: From progressive neoliberalism to Trump and Beyond.* New York: Verso.

Gorbachev, M. (1986). *Speeches and writings.* Oxford and New York: Pergamon.

Harvey, D. (2018). Universal alienation. *TripleC, 16*(2), 424–439. doi: 10.31269/triplec.v16i2.1026

Hrytsenko, A. (2013). Дві різні України [Two different Ukraines]. *Ukrayinska Pravda.* Retrieved from http://blogs.pravda.com.ua/authors/grytsenko/52ae1bbb1e26e

Ishchenko, V. (2020). Insufficiently diverse: The problem of nonviolent leverage and radicalization of Ukraine's Maidan uprising, 2013–2014. *Journal of Eurasian Studies, 11*(2), 201–215. doi: 10.1177/1879366520928363

Judis, J. (2016). *The populist explosion: How the great recession transformed American and European politics.* New York: Columbia Global Reports.

KIIS. (2013, November 26). Which way Ukraine should go—Which union should join. *Kyiv International Institute of Sociology.* Population preferences for two weeks before the Vilnius Summit. Retrieved from http://kiis.com.ua/?lang=eng&cat=reports&id=204&page=2

Knoblock, N. (Ed.). (2020). *Language of conflict: Discourses of the Ukrainian crisis.* London: Bloomsbury Publishing.

Krausz, T. (2007). Perestroika and the redistribution of property in the Soviet Union: Political perspectives and historical evidence. *Contemporary Politics, 13*(1), 3–36. doi: 10.1080/13569770701246195

Mitrokhin, S. (1990). Трактат о толпе [*A treatise on the crowd*]. *Panorama.* Retrieved from http://www.panorama.ru/gazeta/1-30/p21trak.html

Mouffe, C. (2016, April 29). In defense of left-wing populism. *Conversation.* Retrieved from http://theconversation.com/in-defence-of-left-wing-populism-55869

Mykhnenko, V. (2003). State, society and protest under post-Communism: Ukrainian miners and their defeat. In P. Kopecky & C. Mudde (Eds.), *Uncivil society? Contentious politics in post-Communist Europe* (pp. 93–113). New York: Routledge.

Novodvorskaya, V. (1990, September). We refuse collaborating with power. *Orientir,* p. 3.

Phelan, S. (2007). The discourses of neoliberal hegemony: The case of the Irish Republic. *Critical Discourse Studies, 4*(1), 29–48. doi: 10.1080/17405900601149459

Plokhy, S. (2008). *Ukraine and Russia: Representations of the past.* Toronto: University of Toronto Press.

Sakwa, R. (2005). Perestroika and the challenge to democracy in Russia. *Demokratizatsiya, 13*(2), 255–275. doi: 10.3200/DEMO.13.2.255-276

Sakwa, R. (2015). *Frontline Ukraine: Crisis in borderlands.* New York: I. B. Tauris.

Shlapentokh, V. (1993). Privatization debates in Russia: 1989–1992. *Comparative Economic Studies, 35*(2), 19–33.

Siegelbaum, L. (1997). Freedom of prices and the price of freedom: The miners' dilemmas in the Soviet Union and its successor states. *The Journal of Communist Studies and Transition Politics, 13*(4), 1–27. doi: 10.1080/13523279708415358

Sigal, E. (2014, May 26). Петр Порошенко: от сласти к власти [Petro Poroshenko: from sweetness to power]. *Kommersant.* Retrieved from https://www.kommersant.ru/doc/2465569

Snyder, T. (2018). *The road to unfreedom: Russia, Europe, America.* New York: Tim Duggan Books.

Stavrakakis, Y. (2017). Discourse theory in populism research: Three challenges and a dilemma. *Journal of Language and Politics, 16*(4), 523–534. doi: 10.1075/jlp.17025.sta

Swain, A. (2006). Soft capitalism and a hard industry: Virtualism, the "transition industry" and the restructuring of the Ukrainian coal industry. *Transactions of the Institute of British Geographers, 31*(2), 208–223. doi: 10.1111/j.1475-5661.2006.00212.x

Taguieff, P.-A. (2016, June 25). The revolt against the elites, or the new populist wave. *Telos.* Retrieved from https://www.telospress.com/author/pataguieff

Taylor, C. (1992). *Sources of the self: The making of the modern identity.* Cambridge, MA: Harvard University Press.

Turpin, J. (1995). *Reinventing the Soviet self: Media and social change in the former Soviet Union.* Westport, CT: Praeger.

Tymoshenko, Y. (2014). Речь Юлии Тимошенко на Майдане после освобождения из тюрьмы [Yulia Tymoshenko's speech at the Maidan after her release from prison]. *YouTube.* Retrieved from https://www.youtube.com/watch?v=Q57-QIq4mnE

UN OHCHR. (2017). Report on the human rights situation in Ukraine 16 August to 15 November 2017. Retrieved from http://www.ohchr.org/Documents/Countries/UA/UAReport20th_EN.pdf

Usher, K. A. (1998). *Ukraine: Country profile.* London: Economist Intelligence Unit.

Wilson, A. (2014). *Ukraine crisis: What it means for the West.* New York: Yale University Press.

Yekelchuk, S. (2015). *The conflict in Ukraine: What everyone needs to know.* New York: Oxford University Press.

Yurchenko, Y. (2018). *Ukraine and the empire of capital: From marketization to armed conflict.* London: Pluto Press.

Zhuravlev, O., & Ishchenko, V. (2020). Exclusiveness of civic nationalism: Euromaidan eventful nationalism in Ukraine. *Post-Soviet Affairs, 36*(3), 226–245. doi: 10.1080/1060586X.2020.1753460

Žižek, S. (2018). The prospects of radical change today. *TripleC, 16*(2), 476–489. doi: 10.31269/triplec.v16i2.1023

2 Euphemizing the Neoliberal Promise

Mythologizing Capitalism

As outlined in the previous chapter, there is a consensus among many critical thinkers that the global populist explosion came about as a response to people's disillusionment with neoliberal capitalism in all its numerous negative manifestations. The previous chapter also notes that Ukraine was not an exception—ultimately, the success of the anti-oligarchic agenda of Zelensky's populist program (to be discussed in Chapter 3) was conditioned by people's resentment over the consequences of post-Soviet neoliberal reforms resulting in the oligarchic system of power, unequal access to state resources, the dismantling of the welfare system, etc. The disillusionment of Ukrainians with the consequences of the Euromaidan, which also explains Zelensky's victory, was their reaction to the inability of Euromaidan leaders to fulfill their revolutionary promises and destroy the oligarchic political regime, make the system of governance transparent, eradicate corruption, and so forth.

There is, however, one interesting peculiarity that distinguishes the Ukrainian (post-Soviet) situation from that of the West discussed by the critical thinkers briefly reviewed in Chapter 1. Ukrainians were disillusioned with the consequences of Ukraine's post-Soviet neoliberalization, to be sure, yet the various sources of discontent such as the oligarchic system of power, unequal access to state resources, the dismantling of the welfare system, and social and political inequality have commonly been assumed to be part of the specific Ukrainian/post-Soviet situation, rather than local manifestations of the global neoliberal order. An opinion widely shared among Ukrainians (at least, among those who supported the Euromaidan revolution) was that unlike Ukrainian capitalism (though use of the signifier "capitalism" has been extremely rare in public discussions), the Western version has a "human face," to paraphrase Alexander Dubček's famous dictum. As

DOI: 10.4324/9781003228493-3

my analysis of the revolutionary discourse of the Euromaidan shows, the dominant trend was to imagine the West as a coherent mythological object devoid of social problems and contradictions—a symbol of social justice, historical progress, and a finishing line of development—something like an earthly "kingdom of ends" (Baysha, 2016).

From the discursive constructions of Euromaidan activists, Europe, in particular, and the West, in general, appeared as an ideal form of society whose "people are getting richer not on the expense of others" [человек богатеет не за счет других] (Dubrovsky, 2013a), whose politicians were "absolutely fair, responsible, open to public protests, and accountable" [абсолютно чесних, відповідальних, відкритих до майданів і підзвітних] (Bistritsky, 2013), and whose political parties drew their strength from the "ideas coming from people" [ідеї йдуть від народу] (Danylyuk, 2013). As Archbishop Lubomyr Husar, one of the most respected Euromaidan supporters, put it:

> [People] want to live in a society where truth and only truth is circulated, where justice reigns, and where there is a similar interpretation of rights and duties for all citizens, and where everybody gets what s/he needs for a normal life … and—the most important—where human dignity and freedom are spiritual values.
>
> [Люди прагнуть жити в суспільстві, у якому говорять правду і тільки правду, у якому панує справедливість, однакове трактування прав і обов'язків для всіх громадян, у якому кожному віддають те, чого йому потрібно для нормального життя і на що він має право, а головне—у якому духовними цінностями є гідність і свобода людини].
>
> (Husar, 2013)

As my analysis suggests (Baysha, 2016), for many Euromaidan activists, the heaven-on-Earth described by the archbishop existed in Europe. No wonder the refusal to sign the Association Agreement with the EU, which was imagined as a vehicle to bring Ukrainians into the European paradise, was interpreted by many of them as a "catastrophe" [катастрофа] (Matviyenko, 2013) leading to "emptiness" and a "precipice" [пустота, обрыв] (Dubrovsky, 2013b).

In my opinion, which I derive from years of study of the mythologies of capitalism circulating across post-Soviet societies since *perestroika*, such a deeply mythological vision of Western modernity has issued from a specific historical imaginary that has been hegemonized to the point of becoming common sense. According to this hegemonic vision, shared by many Ukrainians, the West (always imagined in universal terms without internal contradictions) has been serving as a model of social justice and the historical avant-garde, leading humanity toward "normal" and just social conditions. It is this sedimented, normalized judgment that has led Ukrainians to believe that getting rid of oligarchs and corruption would allow them to achieve a perfect "Western condition" where social justice, equality, and democracy would reign. Many Ukrainians, although disillusioned with the living conditions brought about by post-Soviet neoliberal reforms, nevertheless tend to blame not neoliberalism/capitalism per se (again, this kind of discourse is extremely marginal in the Ukrainian public sphere), but "distortions" specific to Ukraine. If "corrected," the neoliberal condition in Ukraine would be as good as it is in the West—this has been a normalized judgment among many Ukrainians, especially those who supported the Euromaidan. At the end of the day, it is this belief in universal progress, molded in the Western ideal, that has made the ideology of neoliberalism so successful in post-Soviet terrains.

Despite this important difference in the nuances of disillusionment with the neoliberal order between the West and "the rest" (as represented by Ukraine in this case), there is a similarity that is no less important. As Nancy Fraser's (2019) analysis of "progressive neoliberalism" suggests, neoliberal endeavors in any location have a better chance of being accepted uncritically if repackaged and presented as "progressive."

Progressive Neoliberalism

According to Fraser, what contributed greatly to the hegemony of neoliberal policies within the Western context was the formation of "progressive neoliberalism"—a hegemonic bloc combining "an expropriative, plutocratic economic program with a liberal-meritocratic politics of recognition" (2019, p. 12). "Neoliberals gained power," Fraser (2017) argues, by draping their project in a new cosmopolitan ethos, centered on diversity, women's empowerment, and LGBTQ rights. Drawing in supporters of such ideas, they forged a new hegemonic bloc." In Fraser's (2017) view, neoliberal hegemony was formed through "an alliance of mainstream currents of new social movements (feminism, anti-racism, multiculturalism and LGBTQ rights) on the one side, and high-end 'symbolic' and service-based sectors of business (Wall Street, Silicon Valley and Hollywood) on the other"—an alliance of "progressive forces" and "the forces of cognitive capitalism, especially financialization." "The right-wing 'fundamentalist' version of neoliberalism," Fraser's (2019) argument goes, "could not become hegemonic in a country whose common sense was still shaped by New Deal thinking, the 'rights revolution,' and a slew of social movements descended from the New Left" (p. 12). "For the neoliberal project to triumph," she claims, "it had to be repackaged, given a broader appeal, and linked to other, noneconomic aspirations for emancipation" (Fraser, 2019, p. 13). However unwittingly, Fraser argues, the new social movements enabled such "repackaging" by lending their charisma to the neoliberal project: "Only when decked out as progressive could a deeply regressive political economy become the dynamic center of a new hegemonic bloc," Fraser (2019, p. 13) asserts.

In other words, neoliberalism's ability to mask itself under an attractive progressive cover—to "euphemize itself," as Phelan (2007) put it—was essential to its success. In contrast to a "transparent" neoliberal discourse articulated via an antagonistic relationship between the market and the state, its "euphemized" version adopts a post-political stance by linking to such elements as consensus, inclusiveness, morality, modernization, national good, progress, and so on (Harjuniemi, 2019).

Fraser's argument resonates well with many communication scholars analyzing how neoliberalism euphemizes itself through activating links with "post-political" progressive social struggles; the list of such scholarly works would be rather extensive (e.g., Ashby-King & Hanasono, 2019; Dingo, 2018; Jacobsson, 2019; Jones & Mukherjee, 2010; Orgad & Nikunen, 2015; Roderick, 2019; Tompkins, 2017). These works are in line with Fraser's (2019) description of the "repackaging" of the neoliberal project with unwitting cover from new social movements (p. 13). In discourse studies, Fraser's "repackaging" appears as rearticulation: when "transparent neoliberalism" comes to be articulated as a "euphemized neoliberalism," linked to such elements as "progress," "modernity," "civilization," "emancipation," and so forth.

Despite the resonance of Fraser's theory with broader critical scholarship, it primarily describes U.S. neoliberalism and does not connect with the variety of neoliberal contexts worldwide. While neoliberalism is a global development, there are not so many non-Western societies whose new social movements have the "charisma" to influence public mood. In many places outside Europe and the US, the prevailing public attitudes toward the agendas of new social movements remain intolerant, and their activities can hardly be considered influential or effective enough to "lend charisma" to the neoliberal order. In this sense, despite Fraser's (2019) acknowledgment that "our political crisis… is not just American, but global" (p. 8), her analysis is West-centric.

Nonetheless, this does not make Fraser's line of argument irrelevant to non-Western cultural spaces. If, following Laclau (2005), we consider "progress" as an empty/floating signifier, "progressive neoliberalism" will work even in the context of non-Western societies, albeit in a broader sense not discussed by Fraser. In many non-Western societies, which have their own versions of "local neoliberalisms" (Peck & Theodore, 2019, p. 247), the idea of "progress" may be linked not to the politics of recognition, but to the idea of modernization—economic, technological, and political. Modernization, in turn, may also be articulated differently: as a project of Westernization, which was the case in Yeltsin's Russia or as an "alternative modernity"—"nation as a corporation" in Singapore. These otherwise different versions of "progressive neoliberalism" (in a broadened usage of the term) euphemize their neoliberal programs through the discourse of "progress," in line with Fraser's observation that "only when decked out as *progressive* could a deeply *regressive* political economy become the dynamic center of a new hegemonic bloc" (Fraser & Jaeggi, 2018, p. 202, emphasis original). If we consider "progressive" as an empty/floating signifier (basic concepts of the discourse theory of Laclau and Mouffe, to be presented in the next section) where "progress" is linked to different associations in different sociocultural environments, then the scope of "progressive neoliberalism" may become global.

Empty Signifier: Methodological Foundations

Discourse Theory of Laclau and Mouffe

Laclau and Mouffe's discourse theory (DT) considers discourses from macro-textual and macro-contextual perspectives. In contrast to many other theories of discourse whose focus is on linguistic analysis of micro-contextual situations, DT considers discursive formations at the ideological and societal levels: It is among the theories that are "more concerned with general, overarching patterns and aim at a more abstract mapping of the discourses that circulate in society" (Phillips & Jørgensen, 2002, p. 20). Originally developed in their volume *Hegemony and Socialist Strategy* (*HSS*), DT postulates that social reality is only possible on the condition of "discursivity," where discourse is understood as a "social fabric" on which "social actors occupy different positions" (p. xiii). Articulated through both linguistic and non-linguistic elements, discourse appears as a real force that contributes to the formation and constitution of social relations. Discourse is thus conceptualized as a "structured totality resulting from the articulatory practice," where "articulation" means "any practice establishing relations among elements" (Laclau, 2005, p. 105). Discourses are stabilized by nodal points or "master-signifiers," which assume "a 'universal' structuring function" (Laclau & Mouffe, 1985, p. 98).

Discourse forms when one element from the discursive field—a reservoir of all available signs—assumes the hegemonic representation of a chain of elements related through articulation. A particular element that assumes a hegemonic (synecdochic) representation of the chain of all elements "becomes something of the order of an empty signifier, its own particularity embodying an unachievable fullness" (Laclau, 2005, p. 71). To be sure, this signifier is not completely "empty" because it signifies what, strictly speaking, it is not: an impossible totality of various elements united equivalentially. If used by alternative discourses, the same signifier comes to be linked to alternative chains of equivalence; if this happens, the meaning of such a signifier appears to be "suspended"—it becomes "floating."

Since social relations are seen as discursively constructed, the classical "thought/reality" dichotomy no longer appears relevant, and "the categories which have until now been considered exclusively of one or another" are reconsidered (Laclau & Mouffe, 1985, p. 110). Synonymy, metonymy, metaphor, and other rhetorical devices are understood not as "forms of thought that add a second sense to a primary" but as "part of the primary terrain itself in which the social is constructed" (Laclau & Mouffe, 1985, p. 110). Such ontological generality of rhetoric implies that hegemony—the dominance of a particular meaning established by discourse—appears through the passage from metonymy to metaphor, from a "contiguous" starting point to its consolidation in "analogy" (Laclau, 2014, p. 22).

If presented in the terms of DT, the discursive euphemization of European integration, discussed earlier, happened when the idea of "civilizational progress" with respect to the Euromaidan had displaced other ideas associated with it, first metonymically (i.e., as a contingent substitution), then metaphorically (i.e., as an unquestioned analogy), and finally, synecdochically—in other words, when the empty signifier "progress" assumed the hegemonic representation of the whole chain of equivalence uniting all other nodal points associated with the hegemonic Euromaidan discourse (democracy, justice, law and order, prosperity, economic growth, Westernization, civilization).

In a similar fashion, in the case of Zelensky's land reform (to be discussed in Chapter 6), euphemization took place when the idea of "anti-Communism" had come to displace other ideas associated with the reform—when "anti-Communism" assumed the hegemonic representation of the whole chain of equivalence uniting all other nodal points of the same progressive discourse employed by Euromaidan activists: democracy, justice, law and order, economic growth, prosperity, progress, Westernization, civilization. It is also important to highlight that the nodal points characterizing the land-reform discourse of the opposition—violation of the constitution, financial speculation, Ukraine's colonization, people's impoverishment, the lack of transparency, anti-democracy, etc.—were excluded from the discourse of Zelensky's political party. The euphemization, therefore, was a twofold process of (1) the exclusion of all problematic meanings associated with the reforms, and (2) synecdochical representation of the reforms with an idea that had nothing to do with the essence of the proposed changes.

According to DT, all social meanings or identities (or "totalities," as Laclau and Mouffe call them) are both impossible and necessary: "Impossible, because the tension between equivalence and difference is ultimately insurmountable; necessary, because without some kind of closure, however precarious it might be, there would be no signification and no identity" (Laclau, 2005, p. 70). However, no ultimate fixing of meaning is possible, since any constructed totality (and all totalities are constructed) is "subverted by a field of discursivity which overflows it" (Laclau & Mouffe, 1985, p. 113). These formulations are always precarious and unstable, given the discord between attempts to construct collective identities (or meanings) and the discursive impossibility of their total closures.

Laclau's Theory of Populism

Laclau's theory of populism (2005), developed in his later works, is built on DT's foundations. According to Laclau, populism appears not as an ideology or "a type of movement—identifiable with either a special social base or a particular ideological orientation—but a political logic" (Laclau, 2005, p. 117). It is a "way of constituting the very unity of the group"—"the people" (Laclau, 2005, p. 74). "The people" of a populist movement appear when one unsatisfied popular demand—the smallest unit of his analysis—comes to be united with other demands, and when these demands are "equivalently" united to oppose the established order. "The people" of the Euromaidan appeared when the unsatisfied demands of Euro-romantics, liberals, nationalists, etc., were equivalentially united to oppose Yanukovych's "corrupted regime"; "the people" of Zelensky (to be discussed in Chapter 3) emerged when the incommensurable demands of all Ukrainians were united equiv-alentially and juxtaposed against oligarchs and their puppets, corrupted politicians.

This chain of otherwise different and sometimes even incommensu-rable claims is equivalent only in one sense: vis-à-vis the "otherness" of those excluded from the newly established populist collective (its totality). The exclusion of "otherness" is thus the condition that sets up the emergence of "the people," and thereby enables populism to take root: "To grasp that totality conceptually, we have to grasp its limits—that is to say, we have to differentiate it from something other than itself" (Laclau, 2005, p. 69). This is why the simplification of the social and its Manichean division into "us" vs. "them" are the most readily distinguishable features of populism despite the fact that any populist identity, created through the equivalential chaining of various unsatisfied demands, will necessarily be full of internal contradictions and tensions. All populist totalities, therefore, are formed through the tension of differential and equivalential logics.

According to Laclau (2005), any populist identity requires naming, which is central in constituting the unity of a populist collective: It serves as "a social cement" (Laclau, 2005, p. x) used to assemble the het-erogeneous elements of the impossible but necessary unity. The name of a populist identity thus becomes an empty signifier while playing a cen-tral role in providing unity and identity to a populist collective. Because any assemblage of heterogeneous elements can only be kept together if unified by a single name (an empty signifier), and because "the extreme form of singularity is an individuality" (Laclau, 2005, p. 100), the group as a whole is often identified with the name of its leader. In the populist project of Zelensky (see Chapter 3), the populist identity of his "people" has been kept together by an empty signifier—the phrase "servant of the people," used for both the title of a fictional TV series and a real-life political party—and the "servant" himself, Holoborodko-Zelensky.

The whole process of "investing" one particular signifier with the meaning of "mythical fullness" is unthinkable without "affect"—the moment of "enjoyment" (Laclau, 2005, pp. 101–115). "There is no pop-ulism," Laclau (2005) claims, "without affective investment in a partial object" (p. 116); "pure harmony would be incompatible with affect" (p. 118). When a "popular demand" appears—passionately formed from the plurality of unsatisfied social claims—an internal antagonistic fron-tier emerges, separating the institutionalized system from the people. The social is dichotomized. This division is sustained through the em-ployment of privileged signifiers like "regime" or "oligarchy" to denote the totality of the "evil other" as well as "the people" or "the nation" to denote the "good us."

Laclau argues that any political intervention is populistic to some extent, which "does not mean, however, that all political projects are equally populistic; that depends on the extension of the equivalential chain unifying social demands" (Laclau, 2005, p. 154). The more extended the chain, the more inclusive it is. As Stavrakakis (2017) explains, "In inclusionary populism, the dichotomization of the political space is arranged in a mostly vertical manner (up/down, high/low), while exclusionary populism involves a horizontal (inside/outside) dichotomic arrangement" (p. 530). Usually, inclusivity characterizes left-wing populist parties and movements, while exclusivity is a distinctive feature of right-wing populist forces (Mudde & Kaltwasser, 2013). While the populism of the Euromaidan, dominated by right-wing forces, was exclusionary, Zelensky's populism, uniting all Ukrainians against the oligarchy, is an inclusive one (see Chapter 3).

Many scholars agree that populism is a "thin" ideology: one "whose morphological structure is restricted to a set of core concepts which alone are unable to provide a reasonably broad, if not comprehensive, range of answers to the political questions that societies generate" (Stanley, 2008, p. 99). Because of their conceptual poverty, thin ideologies usually coexist with full ideologies such as liberalism, socialism, communism, and so forth. For this reason, populism can occur anywhere along the ideological spectrum; it may be left-wing, right-wing, or centrist. As De Cleen and colleagues put it, "a populist logic can be invoked to further very different political goals, from radical left to right, or from progressive to regressive" (p. 649). This consideration is useful to keep in mind while analyzing the relationship between populism and neoliberalism, the focus of this book.

Discursive-Material Knot

The idea of contingency is central to DT's conceptualization of discourse: Chains of equivalence may be broken, and their elements may be linked to alternative associations, disrupting established meanings and leading to the formation of new understandings within alternative discourses. Recognizing the contingency of any discursive formation is crucially important because hegemonic policies, with their open-ended horizon of political options, become possible only when social relations are seen as unfixed and unstable. In contrast to closed systems of permanent repetition, where nothing can be hegemonized, open social systems create opportunities for alternative articulations, and thus for hegemonic practices.

The importance of contingency is further emphasized by Nico Carpentier (2017) in his Discursive-Material Knot (DMK), which expands the discourse theory of Laclau and Mouffe to include the material and make analysis of the social richer. This move, in his view, allows "not merely focusing on media talk, for instance, but also on the contextualized processes of discursive-ideological production and their material components" (Carpentier, 2017, p. 5). Such an expansion allows otherwise invisible forces to be recognized, adding contingency to established meanings by destabilizing existing sedimentations and preventing discourses from becoming hermetically closed. The latter allows for discursive struggles and the freedom to identify with some discourses but not with others.

In Carpentier's model, the material appears as both constructive and destructive: It structures the social by providing or denying access to spaces, by allowing or refusing to allow bodies to move, by encouraging or discouraging particular actions and significations, by creating or ruining material and non-material (discursive) structures, and so forth. By the logic of *invitation* and *dislocation*, the material participates in discursive struggles over meanings, suggesting this or that particular articulation. Objects enter the social not only by assuming the role of intermediaries or mediators, but also by acting as social agents of their own and/or as the instruments of power. Any event—a material change—can dislocate discourse because of the inability of the latter to attribute meaning to the former; in such cases, escaping representation, the material destabilizes discourses by pointing to their internal contradictions and their limited capacity to represent the material world.

To increase "the theoretical visibility of the material in the interactions between the discursive and the material," Carpentier (2017, p. 38) employs Deleuze and Guattari's concept of the machine as "a system of interruptions or breaks" "related to a continual material flow ... that it cuts into" (Deleuze & Guattari, 1984, p. 36). Carpentier presents machines not only as material but also as functional assemblages, associating them with humankind through multiple dimensions—material, semiotic, social, representational, and so forth. The material invites particular discourses to become part of the assemblage, while encouraging the production of some or the frustration of others. But the material is also always invested with meaning. Hegemonic orders provide contextual frameworks of intelligibility that intervene in these assemblages. This also implies that discourses impact the production of materials, not only to give meaning to them, but also to co-determine their materiality. The material can disrupt or strengthen discursive orders; however, its invitation may be ignored, and an alternative meaning can be attached to it. To capture the interaction between the material and the discursive—the process of engraining meaning—Carpentier uses the concept of *investment*.

Although Carpentier discusses the material aspects of social reality in great detail, paying careful attention to material objects, bodies, arrangements, and infrastructure through which practices are performed, he does not incorporate digital artifacts into his model. This is not surprising, given that Carpentier's definition of materiality is linked to the notion of matter—his definition of sign as "M/M, Matter and Meaning" (2017, p. 46) corresponds to the traditional view of the material, which associates it with matter. According to this dominant outlook, digital artifacts do not possess materiality because they are not composed of matter and cannot be touched. As the next section demonstrates, however, there are alternative views suggesting that digital artifacts have their own materiality.

Digital Materiality and DMK

Although digital objects occupy an increasingly central place in the reproduction of the social, their materiality is usually neglected on the basis of "intangibility." As Paul Leonardi (2010, p. 3) put it, "You can touch the copper wires or fiber–optic cables over which voice is transmitted… but you can't touch the data packets in which the sounds of voice are encoded." This passage illustrates what is called "the discourse of dematerialization," which frames digital technology in terms of virtuality and disregards its material aspects (Gabrys, 2011). As a result of this hegemonic vision, the materiality of the digital has gone largely unrecognized in the social sciences (Lécuyer & Brock, 2012).

Questioning the dichotomy between the tangible and the intangible that informs the discourse of dematerialization, some scholars have offered an alternative perspective, proposing to look "straight into the core of the materiality upon which our digital world is based" (Marenko, 2015, p. 109). To do so, Betti Marenko (2015) invokes Deleuze and Guattari's (1988) radical/vital/molecular materialism, which postulates "that all things are formed through differentiation and individuation of the same substance" and that "the human and the nonhuman, the subpersonal and the molecular ceaselessly combine and recombine through a myriad of rhizomes, assemblages and machines" (Marenko, 2015, p. 113). It is through these combinations and re-combinations that "collective assemblages" are formed, uniting the animate and the inanimate, the natural and the artificial, the living and the nonliving, the organic and the inorganic.

From this perspective, the interface of any digital device would become "the hinge of the user-device assemblage. By bringing together human sensorium and electronic sensors, the interface mediates the encounter of two different intelligences: the human and the digital" (Marenko, 2015, p. 119). In other words, the interface stops being a self-contained object and transforms into an "objectscape made of distributed materials, bodies, techniques, and practices, some human, and some not"—"a mixture of agencies distributed across analogue and digital territories" (Marenko, 2015, p. 122).

Conflating hardware and software, a radical materialist outlook allows moving through the interface and reaching the essential component of the electronic world, the microchip made of silicon—a material substance. The discourse of the immaterial as applied to the digital world appears to be disrupted by such an outlook. As Jennifer Gabrys (2011) put it,

> The transmission of information into bits, or binary units that correspond to electrical pulses, requires this composite of silicon, chemicals, metals, plastics, and energy. It would be impossible to separate the zeros and ones of information from the firing of these electrical pulses and the processed silicon through which they course.
>
> (p. 24)

According to this radical-molecular perspective, "there is no software; only hardware" (Kittler, 1995), and the digital cannot be comprehended without regard for its materiality.

On the other hand (or rather, on the other side of the interface), the human body, constituting part of a user-device assemblage, participates in the processes of information production and exchange chemically, electrically, and affectively: "Eyes, ears, nose, tongue, skin—these are merely interfaces, ways for a body to chemically convert the uncharged outside world into current that, as it leaps through the brain, creates our thoughts and feelings" (Tingley, 2013). Everything human beings think, feel, and do would be impossible without the work of neurons within the nervous system—also a material substance.

From the perspective of radical molecular materialism, it would therefore be impossible to isolate discourse from complex discursive-material assemblages that mix in various combinations the discursive and the material, the animate and the inanimate, the natural and the artificial, the living and the nonliving, the organic and the inorganic, etc. As the case of Zelensky presented in the next chapter suggests, this perspective may be helpful in analyzing meanings constructed within assemblages of "the virtual" and "the real," i.e., the digital and non-digital aspects of discursive-material knots.

References

Ashby-King, D., & Hanasono, L. (2019). Diverging discourses: Examining how college students majoring in communication define diversity. *Qualitative Research Reports in Communication*, *20*(1), 9–18. doi: 10.1080/17459435.2019.1572645

Baysha, O. (2016). European integration as imagined by Ukrainian Pravda's Bloggers. In M. Pantti (Ed.), *Media and the Ukraine crisis: Hybrid media practices and narratives of conflict* (pp. 71–88). New York: Peter Lang.

Bistritsky, Y. (2013, November 29). Євромайдани—кінець і істина історії противсіхів [Euromaidan—the end and the truth of the history of protivsihs]. *Ukrayinska Pravda*. Retrieved from http://www.pravda.com.ua/columns/2013/11/29/7003584

Carpentier, N. (2017). *The discursive-material knot: Cyprus in conflict and community media participation.* New York: Peter Lang.

Danylyuk, T. (2013, November 27). Двічі в одну річку не ввійдеш? Памфлет для Розчарованих Помаранчевою Революцією [Cannot enter the river twice? A pamphlet for the disappointed by the Orange Revolution]. *Ukrayinska Pravda*. Retrieved from http://www.pravda.com.ua/columns/2013/11/27/7003207

De Cleen, B., Glynos, J., & Mondon, A. (2018). Critical research on populism: Nine rules of engagement. *Organization*, *25*(5), 649–661. doi 10.1177/1350508418768053

Deleuze, G., & Guattari, F. (1984). *Anti-Oedipus: Capitalism and schizophrenia.* London: Athlone Press.

Deleuze, G., & Guattari, F. (1988). *A thousand plateaus. Capitalism and schizophrenia.* London: Athlone Press.

Dingo, R. (2018). Speaking well: The benevolent public and rhetorical production of neoliberal political economy. *Communication and the Public*, *3*(3), 232–246. doi: 10.1177/2057047318794964

Dubrovsky, V. (2013a, November 26). Політекономія патріотизму [The political economy of patriotism]. *Ukrayinska Pravda*. Retrieved from http://www.pravda.com.ua/columns/2013/11/26/7003071

Dubrovsky, V. (2013b, December 1). Точка біфуркації [The point of bifurcation]. *Ukrayinska Pravda*. Retrieved from http://www.pravda.com.ua/columns/2013/12/1/7003965

Fraser, N. (2017, September 21). Against progressive neoliberalism, a new progressive popu lism. *Southern Social Movements Newswire*. Retrieved from https://www.cetri.be/Against-Progressive-Neoliberalism?lang=fr

Fraser, N. (2019). *The old is dying and the new cannot be born: From progressive neoliberalism to Trump and beyond.* New York: Verso.

Fraser, N., & Jaeggi, R. (2018). *Capitalism: A conversation in critical theory.* New York: John Wiley & Sons.

Gabrys, J. (2011). *Digital rubbish: A natural history of electronics.* Ann Arbor: University of Michigan Press.

Harjuniemi, T. (2019). The Economist's depolitisation of European austerity and the constitution of a "euphemized" neoliberal discourse. *Critical Discourse Studies, 17*(5), 494–509. doi: 10.1080/17405904.2019.1649162

Husar, L. (2013, November 11). Працюйте і моліться! [Work and pray!]. *Ukrayinska Pravda.* Retrieved from http://www.pravda.com.ua/columns/2013/12/11/7006408

Jacobsson, D. (2019). In the name of (un)sustainability: A critical analysis of how neoliberal ideology operates through discourses about sustainable progress and equality. *TripleC, 17*(1), 19–37. doi: 10.31269/triplec.v17i1.1057

Jones, B., & Mukherjee, R. (2010). From California to Michigan: Race, rationality, and neoliberal governmentality. *Communication and Critical/Cultural Studies, 7*(4), 401–422. doi: 10.1080/14791420.2010.523431

Kittler, F. (1995). There is no software. *CTheory.net.* Retrieved from www.ctheory.net/articles.aspx?id=74

Laclau, E. (2005). *On populist reason.* New York: Verso.

Laclau, E. (2014). *The rhetorical foundations of society.* New York: Verso.

Laclau, E., & Mouffe, C. (1985). *Hegemony and socialist strategy: Towards a radical democratic politics.* London: Verso.

Lécuyer, C., & Brock, D. C. (2012). Digital foundations. The making of silicon-gate manufacturing technology. *Technology and Culture, 53*(3), 561–597. doi: 10.1353/tech.2012.0122

Leonardi, P. M. (2010). Digital materiality? How artifacts without matter, matter. *First Monday, 15*(6), 1–20. doi: 10.5210/fm.v15i6.3036

Marenko, B. (2015). Digital materiality, morphogenesis, and the intelligence of the technological object. In E. Marenko & J. Brasset (Eds.), *Deleuze & Design* (pp. 107–129). Edinburg: Edinburg University Press.

Matviyenko, K. (2013, December 6). Щоб Майдан стояв і переміг [Let the Maidan stay and win]. *Ukrayinska Pravda.* Retrieved from http://www.pravda.com.ua/columns/2013/12/6/7005182/

Mudde, C., & Kaltwasser, C. R. (2013). Exclusionary vs. inclusionary populism: Comparing contemporary Europe and Latin America. *Government and Opposition, 48*(2), 147–174. doi: 10.1017/gov.2012.11

Orgad, S., & Nikunen, K. (2015). The humanitarian makeover. *Communication and Critical/Cultural Studies, 12*(3), 229–251. doi: 10.1080/1479 1420.2015.1044255

Peck, J., & Theodore, N. (2019). Still Neoliberalism? *South Atlantic Quarterly, 118*(2), 245–265.

Phelan, S. (2007). The discourses of neoliberal hegemony: The case of the Irish Republic. *Critical Discourse Studies, 4*(1), 29–48. doi: 10.1080/17405 900601149459

Phillips, L., & Jørgensen, M. (2002). *Discourse analysis as theory and method.* London: Sage.

Roderick, I. (2019). Neoliberal multiculturalism and the discourse of primitivism at Walt Disney World's Pandora. *Journal of Multicultural Discourses*, *14*(3), 195–207. doi: 10.1080/17447143.2019.1588898

Stanley, B. (2008). The thin ideology of populism. *Journal of Political Ideologies*, *13*(1), 95–110. doi: 10.1080/13569310701822289

Stavrakakis, Y. (2017). Discourse theory in populism research: Three challenges and a dilemma. *Journal of Language and Politics*, *16*(4), 523–534. doi: 10.1075/jlp.17025.sta

Tingley, K. (2013). The body electric. A scientist takes computing power under the skin. *New Yorker.* Retrieved from http://www.braemarenergy.com/news/media/2013/bodyelectric_newyorker_1125.html

Tompkins, J. (2017). "It's about respect!" College-athlete activism and left neoliberalism. *Communication and Critical/Cultural Studies*, *14*(4), 351–368. doi: 10.1080/14791420.2017.1348610

3 The People vs. The Elites

From Comedian to President

The story of Zelensky-the-president started on April 30, 2019, when he inflicted a crushing defeat on then-incumbent President Poroshenko by receiving 73.2 percent of the popular vote in the second round of the presidential election. To many observers, Zelensky's amazing ascent to power came as a shock: Widely known as a comic actor ridiculing the political establishment of Ukraine, he was a complete newbie in professional politics.

Zelensky is what might be called a "self-made man." He was born on January 25, 1978, in an ordinary Soviet family: The father of the future president was a university mathematics teacher and his mother was an engineer. The family resided in Kryvyi Rih—a city in the southeast of Ukraine known not only for its iron-ore mines and huge metallurgical plants but also for a high crime rate. The site of Zelensky's childhood was "a bandit city, a city of the 1990s" [бандитский город, город 1990], as Zelensky acknowledged in one of his interviews (Zelensky, 2019c, 00:03–00:06). By saying "a city of the 1990s," he was referring to having grown up during the first decade of Ukraine's independence, a time characterized by massive unemployment and rampant delinquency—the consequences of the dissolution of the Soviet welfare system and the beginning of neoliberal reforms. From 1995 to 2000, Volodymyr attended Kryvyi Rih Economic Institute. Although he graduated with a license to practice law, Zelensky has never worked as a lawyer. During his studies, he became an actor with a student theater and developed the skills from which his successful career as a comedian began. After graduation, he co-founded the production studio "Kvartal-95," which later became one of the most successful showbusiness companies not only in Ukraine but also throughout the entire former Soviet Union.

DOI: 10.4324/9781003228493-4

For a comedian such as Zelensky to transform his showbusiness success into political capital is not unique. Suffice it to mention Patrick Layton Paulsen, known for his satirical campaigns for President of the US; Lord Buckethead, who ran for British parliament against Margaret Thatcher, John Major, and Theresa May; or Jón Gnarr, who served as the Mayor of Reykjavík. Examples of political parties established by comedians are even more common: the Rhinoceros Party of Canada promising "to keep none of its promises," the Anarchistic Pogo Party of Germany advocating for youth pensions, the Vrije Socialistische Groep of the Netherlands nominating homeless people for political office, and so forth. Usually, however, "joke" parties organized by comedians receive only a modicum of actual support from voters. Typically, such parties attempt to challenge normalized assumptions and suggest alternative ways of looking at the familiar problems of capitalist states.

By contrast, the election platform of Zelensky's party, *Servant of the People*—named after the title of his TV show and launched only a year prior to Zelensky's dizzying electoral success—was explicitly West-oriented. It promised that, under the leadership of the "servants," Ukraine would be "normalized" according to Western standards. Among its goals were to:

Decentralize power in accordance with European norms [Проведемо децентралізацію влади відповідно до європейських норм],

Turn public administrations into prefectures of the European type [Перетворимо державні адміністрації на префектури європейського типу],

Create a National Economic Strategy with a key goal—to achieve higher than the average European level of income and quality of life for Ukrainians [Створимо Національну економічну стратегію з ключовою метою—досягти вищого за середньоєвропейський рівня доходів та якості життя українців],

Adopt the laws necessary for the implementation of the Association Agreement between Ukraine and the EU [Ухвалимо закони, необхідні для виконання Угоди про Асоціацію між Україною та ЄС],

Expand cooperation with the EU and NATO [розширення співпраці з Євросоюзом і НАТО],

Reform the armed forces in accordance with NATO standards [реформування Збройних сил за стандартами НАТО] (Program, n/d), and so forth.

With this West-centric platform, Zelensky and his party targeted those dispossessed not by capitalist globalization, but by the "abnormality" of Ukrainian capitalism (though the word "capitalism" has certainly never been mentioned), which they were going to align with Western standards. During his inaugural presidential speech of May 20, 2019, Zelensky declared:

> We have chosen a path to Europe, but Europe is not somewhere out there. Europe is here (in the head—Ed.). And after it appears here, it will be everywhere, all over Ukraine.
>
> [Ми обрали шлях до Європи, але Європа—не десь там. Європа ось тут (у голові—ред.). І коли вона буде ось тут—тоді вона з'явиться і ось тут—у всій Україні].
>
> (Zelensky, 2019a)

In this speech, Zelensky quoted a famous saying from Ronald Reagan, whom he called "cool":

> Allow me to quote one American actor who has become a cool American president: "The government does not solve our problems. The government is our problem."
>
> [Дозвольте мені процитувати одного американського актора, який став класним американським президентом: «Уряд не вирішує наших проблем. Уряд і є нашою проблемою»].
>
> (Zelensky, 2019a)

Reagan's neoliberal formula, proclaimed by Zelensky from the parliamentary tribune on the first day of his presidency, could hardly signal the advent of anything but new neoliberal experiments, as Ukrainians would soon have a chance to realize.

The new government of Ukraine was formed on August 29, 2019. In a meeting with its members just three days later, on September 2, Zelensky instructed Prime Minister Oleksiy Honcharuk to review the existing list of strategic enterprises not subject to privatization by October 1, transfer about 500 state enterprises of the State Property Fund for small privatization by December 1, draft a bill to abolish the moratorium on the sale of agricultural land, and work out a new Land Code by October, with the Verkhovna Rada to adopt it by December (Zelensky, 2019b). Four days later, on September 6, David Arakhamia, the leader of the "servant" parliamentary faction which now had an absolute majority of seats, announced that on a daily basis they would adopt seven to ten laws necessary for Ukraine's "normalization"— accelerating government into "a turbo regime," as he put it (UNIAN, 2019).

The pace of the reforms turned out to be "turbo," indeed. On September 25, a bill establishing a legislative framework for the introduction of market circulation of agricultural land, approved by the government, was registered in the parliament of Ukraine. Additionally, the governmental program, published on September 29, informed Ukrainians that:

> More than a thousand inefficient enterprises will be liquidated— the state will no longer spend taxpayers' funds to support inefficient unprofitable enterprises.

> [Понад тисячу неефективних підприємств буде ліквідовано— держава більше не буде витрачати кошти платників податків на підтримку неефективних збиткових підприємств].
> (Government Program, 2019, p. 49)

The program also boasted that:

> In 5 years, at least 70% of state higher education institutions in Ukraine will leave the status of budgetary institutions.

> [За 5 років не менш як 70% державних закладів вищої освіти вийдуть із статусу бюджетної установи].
> (Government Program, 2019, p. 12)

On October 3, 2019, the parliament approved significant reductions of fines for employers over violations of labor laws. One week later, on October 10, Zelensky announced during a meeting with journalists that the new Labor Code would simplify the dismissal of workers. As usual, he framed the issue in terms of modernization, as a matter of doing away with a relic from bygone Soviet times (more on this in Chapter 6):

> We will not have the Soviet labor code, but the labor code of an independent country. A modern one.

> [В нас буде не Радянський трудовий кодекс. У нас буде трудовий кодекс незалежної країни. Сучасний].
> (Zelensky, 2019d, 1:21:49–1:21:52)

Predictably, trade unions saw the proposed law in a completely different light. It "would seriously undermine fundamental workers' rights," they argued (IndustriAll, 2020).

Right after the formation of the new Ukrainian government and its first steps toward neoliberal reforms in Ukraine, Fitch Ratings, a leading Wall Street firm, upgraded Ukraine's debt rating from B- to B, characterizing the members of the new Ukrainian government as "technocratic, pro-Western, and reform-minded ministers" (RFE/RL, 2019). Other global advocates of neoliberalism were also pleased with such zeal among the "servants." As Zelensky himself acknowledged with a satisfied smile,

> I have been told by everyone—Europeans, the IMF, the EBRD, and the World Bank… All of them are very happy, even saying, let's slow down a little.
>
> [Мені казали всі—і європейці, і Міжнародний Валютний Фонд, і працівники ЄБРР і Світового Банку. Всі дуже задоволені, навіть кажуть, давайте трішечки повільніше].
>
> (Zelensky, 2019e, 1:42–1:53)

Yet there were many who did not seem very happy—a growing body of Ukrainian citizens. As early as in September 2019, it became clear that many of the initiatives put forward by the "servants" were not popular among Ukrainians, especially the land reform: According to various polls, the overwhelming majority (up to 72 percent) opposed lifting the moratorium on land sales (KIIS, 2019). This did not prevent the new party from attempting the move, however. On November 13, 2019, the Ukrainian parliament approved in the first reading the bill on abolishing the moratorium on the sale of agricultural land. The necessity of land sales was also framed in terms of moving away from the non-modern, Soviet condition, toward the normality of capitalism (more on this in Chapter 6).

The unpopular neoliberal reforms initiated by Zelensky, combined with the ongoing war in Donbas that he promised to stop, the lack of criminal cases against corrupt officials and oligarchs whom he promised to imprison, as well as industrial decline, salaries in arrears, budget shortfalls, rising unemployment and catastrophic rates of labor migration and depopulation, [1] plus various scandals inside Zelensky's party— all these factors fomented massive levels of discontent. In September 2019, 57 percent of Ukrainians believed that events in Ukraine were developing in the right direction; in October, this figure was down to 45 percent; in November, it was 37.5 percent (Razumkov Center, 2019). With the advent of the new year, Zelensky's personal approval rating fell below 50 percent, while the rating of his party was 10 percent lower (KIIS, 2020). As of this writing in early August 2021, Zelensky's approval rating is 29 percent (in June 2021, it was 34 percent); the rating of his party is 21 percent among those who will definitely vote and 14 percent among all Ukrainians. Most Ukrainians—69 percent (in June, this number was 64 percent)—believe the country is headed in the wrong direction (KIIS, 2021).

Amid flagging popularity, Zelensky led a major government shake-up on March 4, 2020, ousting his prime minister and several other Cabinet members connected with global financial capital (more on this in Chapter 8). Some observers expressed hope that Zelensky's move to break with pro-Western officials would mean the termination of his neoliberal economic reforms. This was not the case. The adoption of the law on the opening of the land market during an extraordinary parliamentary meeting, convened as an exception to a coronavirus lockdown while Ukrainians could not protest, was the most obvious symbol of the immutability of his course. On March 30, 2020, in his speech preceding the vote, Zelensky (2020) pronounced:

> It is very important for us to sign a memorandum with the International Monetary Fund. And you know perfectly well that the two main conditions are the law on land and the law on banking.
>
> [Для нас дуже важливо, щоб дійсно відбулося підписання Меморандуму з Міжнародним Валютним Фондом. І ви прекрасно знаєте, що дві головні умови—це закон про землю і банківський закон].
>
> (2:37:44–2:38:01)

There is nothing euphemized in this construction, in which Ukraine appears subordinated to the IMF and its neoliberal agenda. If Zelensky had been offering such a vision during his election campaign, it is likely that he would never have won the presidency. But his electoral promise, presented through his TV show *Servant of the People*, was different.

Holoborodko and His People

The first episode of the first season of *Servant of the People* was aired by 1+1, a popular television channel, in fall 2015; the third season came out right before the presidential election, in the spring of 2019. The main character of the series is Vasyl Petrovych Holoborodko, a history teacher whose life changes abruptly after his emotional, obscenity-filled rant about Ukrainian politics appears on the Internet. Holoborodko is mad about the electoral simulacrum in which politicians run campaigns full of phony promises to solve people's problems, while people pretend not to see through the artifice and vote repeatedly for the same crooks. "Fuck privileges!" [льготы ваши на хуй] he shouts, promising that if he could rule the country for just one week, he would "make the teacher live as the president, and the president live as the teacher" [простой бы учитель жил, как president, а president как учитель] (*Servant of the People*, 2016, 12:51–13:04).

This cry from the heart of Holoborodko-the-teacher happens to be heard by millions. Secretly recorded, it is uploaded to social networks by Holoborodko's students who also organize crowdfunding, and millions of viewers collect the necessary sum of money to register Holoborodko as a "people's" presidential candidate. With 76 percent of the popular vote, he wins the presidency in a landslide. It takes 51 episodes for Holoborodko, a young divorced man living with his parents in an old apartment building in the center of Kyiv, to fulfill his promise. He manages to transform Ukraine into a prosperous country where politicians serve the interests of the citizens and where people from all over the world come to settle down in search of a better life.

Unlike the hegemonic discourse of the Euromaidan, which equated "the people" of Ukraine with the supporters of the revolution, whose radical outside was not only Yanukovych's regime but also its "boot-lickers" (anti-Maidan Ukrainians—see Chapter 1), *Servant of the People* portrays the people of Ukraine as an unproblematic totality devoid of internal splits, from which only oligarchs and corrupted politicians/officials are excluded. In Holoborodko's view, Ukraine will become a great country when Ukrainians will stop "measuring each other by patriotism and dividing people into friends and foes but unite" [Мы перестанем мериться патриотизмом, делить украинцев на своих и чужих, а наоборот объединимся] (*Servant of the People*, 2017b, 24:11–24:26).

Holoborodko pronounces these words in an address to the nation in the show's second season. In the closing episodes, which aired right before the actual election of 2019, Holoborodko appeals to the show's fictionalized Ukraine with a similar message: "It makes no difference which language we speak" [I немає ніякої різниці, якою мовою ти спілкуєшся]. If Ukrainians want to keep their country united, he argues, they "need to live humanely and respect each other" [нужно жить по-человечески, хоть как-то уважая друг друга] (*Servant of the People*, 2019c, 40:03–40:19). While delivering this speech, Holoborodko changes languages, pronouncing some phrases in Ukrainian and others in Russian; later, Zelensky would do the same during his actual inaugural speech. By constructing "the people of Ukraine" in this way, Zelensky-Holoborodko explicitly challenged the hegemonic discourse of the Euromaidan that had equated "Ukrainians" with "Maidan supporters." He did away with the link between patriotism and allegiance to the Maidan or nationalism, replacing it with a new link between patriotism and multiculturalism.[2] By doing so, Zelensky-Holoborodko included in his populist equivalential chain not only Maidan supporters and not only Ukrainian-speakers but also all the cultural groups of Ukraine, and he did this with passion—with "an affective investment," to use Laclau's (2005) term.

The culminating "moment of enjoyment" (Laclau, 2005, pp. 111–115) happens in the last episode of the series. Ukraine, once broken into many "states," unifies again. Only two regions, at the far west and the far east of the country, remain "independent." The former is referred to as "the Galician Kingdom" and the latter as "the USSR"—a jab at the radicals on both sides of Ukraine's cultural split for their supposed historical backwardness. During the final episode, there is a major accident in a mine in "the Galician Kingdom": 50 miners are trapped beneath the earth, and only specialists from "the USSR" can save them, because it would take too long for rescue teams from other states to arrive. However, the leader of "the USSR"—its "Secretary General"—forbids anyone to help "the Kingdom" under the threat of life imprisonment. The leaders of "the Kingdom" also refuse to ask "the USSR" for help, despite frantic requests from the miners: "There are also people in Donbas! They will understand!" [На Донбасі теж люди! Вони зрозуміють] (*Servant of the People*, 2019c, 43:50–44:01).

The leader of "the Kingdom" remains unmoved and suggests inviting rescuers from anywhere else—the US, China, India, but definitely not from "the USSR." In the most dramatic moment of the negotiation, specialists from "the USSR," in violation of the "Secretary General's" order, arrive at the scene, whereupon "Kingdom" miners overthrow their leader who tries to prevent "aliens" from entering the territory of the "independent state." Ukrainians from the east and the west re-unite to the sound of sublime music. Ukrainian-speaking westerners say "thank you" in Russian, and Russian-speaking easterners reply in Ukrainian: "We are in this together" [одну справу робимо] (*Servant of the People*, 2019c, 45:02–45:04).

The re-unification of Ukraine under the leadership of Holoborodko invests Ukrainian society with "mythical fullness" (Laclau, 2005, pp.

111–115). Appealing to the nation, he calls on Ukrainians to "change the course of history" [изменить ход истории] "in the name of our future. Our children. Our grandchildren. Future generations" [Во имя нашего будущего. Во имя наших детей. Наших внуков. Будущих поколений] (*Servant of the People*, 2019c, 54:10–54:45). Holoborodko-Zelensky pronounces these words to uplifting music; his face is solemn; his eyes shine. The affective investment is complete: The people's president comes to represent the impossible totality of the Ukrainian people with all their incommensurable aspirations and cultural divides. Corrupted elites and radicals are excluded; they are portrayed as an outside of Ukrainians.

The final words of the show, appearing slowly on the screen before the closing credits, state that Ukrainians cannot "choose either country, language or time of birth" [нам не дано выбирать ни страну, ни язык, ни время рождения], but they can choose "to be human beings" [у нас один выбор—быть людьми] (*Servant of the People*, 2019c, 56:08–56:18). The signature after these final words, delivered right before the actual presidential election of 2019, indicates that their author is Vasyl Petrovych Holoborodko—the founding father of the new nation born from the ruins of the post-Soviet oligarchic order.

The Constitutive Outside

The constructed chain of equivalence uniting the west and the east of the country despite their profound differences in cultural backgrounds and political predispositions becomes possible through the drawing of a strict antagonistic frontier between "working people" who are unified by being "in this together" and their radical outside: "elites" depicted as parasites who consume the fruits of the people's labor. Easily discernable in this construction are traces of the Leninist doctrine of "proletarian internationalism"—a common-sense assumption shared by many people living in the territories of the former USSR. Zelensky-Holoborodko exploits this deeply engrained social sentiment, but in this case the antagonistic frontier does not separate "the people" from "bourgeoisie"; rather, it separates them only from corrupted politicians and oligarchs reaping profits from their control over the political field.

It turns out to be these villains who benefit from and willfully exacerbate the cultural dissimilarities between Ukrainian regions. "You will submit a language bill," an oligarch instructs his parliamentary puppet. "Those speaking the occupant's language cannot call themselves Ukrainians" [Отнесешь законопроект о запрете русского языка: Той хто спілкується на мові окупанта, не може називати себе українцем] (*Servant of the People*, 2019b, 23:18–23:44).

The series depicts each of the oligarchs financing radicals on both sides of the divide: Ukrainian-speaking nationalists and Russian-speaking separatists. In one scene, a separatist and a nationalist are shown together in the office of their oligarchic financier. The former suggests to the latter that they need not attack each other in private, because they are "suckle the same tit" [от одной сиськи кормимся] (*Servant of the People*, 2017d, 3:48–3:56). This and similar scenes from the show suggest that linguistic and cultural differences across Ukrainian regions are not genuinely significant. It is oligarchs and their puppets who create artificial splits along regional lines—a continuing theme throughout all three seasons of the show.

Beyond just the country's radicals, all political parties in Ukraine are shown to be the puppets of oligarchs. At the smallest oligarchic whim, day or night, the parties gather in the parliamentary building to vote as instructed. Under cover of night, deputies show up in the session room dressed in nightgowns, bathrobes, beach attire, hunting outfits, and other inappropriate garments. Three parliamentary factions vote unanimously if three ruling oligarchs agree; if not, faction leaders announce the law to be "against the interests of the Ukrainian people" and threaten to leave the parliamentary coalition. Deputies endlessly fight and hurl insults at each other, but this is only a spectacle, a simulacrum. Behind the scenes, ostensibly implacable ideological opponents are fond of each other, or in one case more than just fond—two of the faction leaders have sex in the house of parliament right before a session at which they harshly attack each other. Their intimate banter is full of political terminology twisted into sexual innuendo: To "make a coalition" [создать коалицию] means to have sexual intercourse, while having "enough votes" and "a big electorate" [А у вас голосов хватит? У меня большой электорат] are taken as references to sexual stamina and physical endowment, etc. (*Servant of the People*, 2017a, 21:18–21:30).

The sexual scene in the house of parliament is very typical not only in terms of its humor, which—as in many other scenes—is achieved through double entendre, but also in its reference to a real romance between two well-known Ukrainian politicians who were political opponents in public and, as rumor had it, lived together in private. All the other characters also have clear references to real figures in Ukrainian politics, with the most obvious match being between the show's faction leader Zhanna Borisenko and Yulia Tymoshenko, the real-life former prime minister known for her love of high-fashion clothing. A scene in the third season, when Zhanna happens to serve temporarily as the president of Ukraine, starts with her scolding subordinates. "Everything is crooked, askew, out of balance!" [все криво косо, никакого баланса] she shouts, accusing subordinates of "jeopardizing the country's budget" [Вы срываете бюджет страны!] (*Servant of the People*, 2019b, 14:12–14:38). The immediate impression is that Zhanna is concerned with the country's budget law. The prolongation of her rant, however, reveals the humor of the situation: "How can I appear at a Cabinet meeting in this?" [Как я могу появиться на заседании Кабинета Министров вот в этом?] shouts Zhanna, throwing dress sketches into the faces of the subordinates, who turn out to be fashion designers. "I am the face of the state, and you dress me like a hooker!" [Я лицо государства, а вы меня одеваете, как профурсетку!] (*Servant of the People*, 2019b, 14:40–14:49).

In another scene, Zhanna shouts at her assistant about the need to seize her last chance to run for president, arguing that by the next election in five years' time she will be "a decrepit old woman with a stick from Dolce and Gabbana" [дряхлой старухой с клюкой от Дойче и Габбана] (*Servant of the People*, 2019a, 58:50–59:03). As in most other scenes involving corrupted and self-absorbed politicians (and there is no other type of politician in the show), the effect of investing them with the meaning of parasites sucking blood from Ukraine's body is achieved by means of humor. Making fun of "the people's exploiters" places these powerful figures in an object-position and creates a cathartic moment of enjoyment shared by the viewers—the people of Ukraine.

The parallels between other figures in Ukrainian politics and show characters are not always direct, but the real situations are easily recognizable. In real life, it was Tymoshenko who used a wheelchair while wearing high-heeled shoes; in the show, a male faction leader is in a wheelchair to feign illness, and his appearance strikingly resembles that of another actual politician. The interchangeability of characters and their prototypes suggests an unequivocal conclusion: Liars and fakers of all kinds manage Ukraine, both in the show and in real life, where the former simply mirrors the latter. The character of the ousted "president" shown in the first episode of the series is representative in this respect. Appearing as a miserable drunkard accustomed to a luxurious life, he cries to Yura, a henchman for the oligarchs, over his electoral defeat by Holoborodko, unable to believe that the people have "stolen" "his country" in which he "ate and drank" [У меня украли страну, Юра!... Я жил в ней, ел в ней, пил в ней!] (*Servant of the People*, 2015, 13:18–13:36). He begs Yura to get him control over lucrative regions in Ukraine to profit from their exploitation: Transcarpathia, Odessa port, etc. [Дайте мне Закарпатье! Порт одесский дайте!] (*Servant of the People*, 2015, 24:32–24:36). This funny scene, which is played very convincingly by an actor, clearly refers to the pre-Maidan President

Yanukovych who was clinging to power and hiding in his fancy country estate while Maidan protesters were dying in the center of Kyiv.

The "realism" of all these and endless similar scenes resonated well with the Ukrainian people's contempt and hatred for the country's political "elites," whom many believed to be accurately depicted in the show. Before the presidential election of 2019, opinion polls showed a "lowest-in-the-world rate of 9% of Ukrainians have confidence in their government" (Bikus, 2019). In the show's representation of ordinary people, politicians appeared as "thieves" [воры] coming to get their hands on people's property, insatiable "rats" [крысы] always wanting more, "a horde" [орда] collecting tribute, and so forth.

When Holoborodko finally gets a chance to reform the system of power in Ukraine, his Minister of Finance (who happens to be his ex-wife) boasts at a Cabinet meeting that they "have got rid of fools" [от дураков, я надеюсь, мы избавились] (*Servant of the People*, 2019c, 34:58–35:03). By "fools," she means politicians, of course. Not only are these figures corrupted, they are also primitively stupid. The series provides endless illustrations of the idiocy of politicians.

Antagonistic Frontier

To define the situation in Laclau's (2005) terms, *Servant of the People* draws a solid antagonistic frontier separating "the people" and "the elites." The latter are not part of the national body, but rather parasites sapping its strength. The equivalential chain of elements characterizing them includes stupidity, hypocrisy, venality, greed, unscrupulousness, gluttony, lust, etc.—nothing positive or redeeming, and there is no chance to work together with such people to reform Ukraine. The country becomes healthy only after getting rid of both oligarchs and their puppets. In the show, some of those who "used to make good money without working" [кто привык нормально зарабатывать, не работая] (*Servant of the People*, 2019c, 37:10–37:14) are imprisoned or flee the country; their property is confiscated. Others—450,000 bureaucrats—find themselves fired.

Referring to his evolution from a "a soft and principled teacher" [мягкого, принципиального учителя] to a "tough" and "unprincipled" president [жесткий, если хотите, беспринципный президент], Holoborodko publicly admits that he has "staged a coup in the country" [мы устроили в стране переворот]. "If I do something wrong," he says, addressing corrupted "others," "the people will tell me. But definitely not you" [Если я сделаю что-то не так, об этом мне скажет народ. Но точно не вы.] (*Servant of the People*, 2017c, 22:30–22:53). In the clearest possible way, this excerpt from the second season illustrates the Manichean division of the Ukrainian social into two non-overlapping entities: "good us" ("the people") vs. "bad them" (corrupted elites).[3] By saying "we staged a coup," Holoborodko acknowledges that imprisonments and property confiscations have been carried out in an extrajudicial manner—skipping the courts is seen as an unavoidable necessity, as all of the judges in the series turn out to be corrupted as well.

In this dirty political environment, Holoborodko-the-president has no other choice but to rely on his old friends, whom he appoints to ministerial positions, to take charge of punishing all the crooked scoundrels without regard to legality. Later, Zelensky-the-president, in the spirit of his show, would also surround himself with old acquaintances and friends to help him carry out his civilizational mission of "normalizing" Ukraine by bringing it up to the neoliberal standards. Thirty such people received state positions after Zelensky came to power, according to the Committee of Voters (2020):

> These people were appointed to the positions of assistants, deputies, heads of the Office of the President, received positions in the security bodies of Ukraine, in the central bodies of executive power, became members of supervisory councils, committees and people's deputies of Ukraine.

> [Вказані особи були призначені на посади помічників, заступників, керівників Офісу Президента, отримали посади в органах безпеки України, в центральних органах виконавчої влади, стали членами наглядових рад, комітетів, були обрані на посади народних депутатів України].

It is noteworthy that "the vast majority of these people have not previously worked in similar positions" [абсолютна більшість з них раніше не працювали на аналогічних посадах], as the Committee of Voters (2020) claims. In other words, they had no relevant experience for performing their new governmental duties—precisely as in the show.

What is probably much more important than his appointing of friends is that in the spring of 2021, with his popularity in a nosedive, Zelensky also imitated Holoborodko by using questionable methods of dealing with "the enemies of the people"—politicians and oligarchs (at least, some of them) who were sanctioned (deprived of their citizens' rights) through a decision handed down by the National Security and Defense Council (NSDC). It is noteworthy that among the first to be sanctioned were two parliamentary deputies from the Opposition Platform "For Life"

(OPZZh), the main political rival of the "servants." By sanctioning opposition politicians by extrajudicial means and shutting down opposition television channels controlled by them—an effective method of silencing the opposition and diminishing its presence in the public sphere—Zelensky was able to improve his rating marginally (although not for long) at the expense of significantly deteriorating the overall quality of the country's democratic condition. The next chapter will discuss this in more detail.

Notes

1 According to a 2019 survey, 55 percent of Ukrainian residents named mass emigration as the greatest threat to the country. The UN estimates that Ukraine could lose nearly a fifth of its population by 2050 (Edwards, 2020).

2 Later, when acting as the real president of Ukraine, Zelensky made a strong shift toward the nationalistic agenda of Poroshenko. When discussing the sympathy of Donbas residents toward Russia, for example, he advised them to immigrate there (Zelensky, 2021).

3 Interestingly, in the first season of the series, the dichotomy was far less strict: "The people" appeared indifferent to the cynicism of the political spectacle in which they were involved, and willingly reproduced the culture of corruption that had permeated all spheres of Ukrainian social life. As the story develops, the leitmotif of the broad culture of corruption vanishes and the focus shifts exclusively to elites, presented as a monolithic group of corrupted and stupid creatures, juxtaposed against ordinary Ukrainians, imagined in similarly monolithic but positive terms. Presumably, the show's original approach was adopted because Zelensky (not to be confused with Holoborodko) initially had no plans to run for president (Antonova, 2019) and could afford, therefore, to interpret Ukrainian social reality in more nuanced, non-populist terms. It is only after he made up his mind to participate in the election that the strategic necessity of employing a more populist discourse emerged.

References

Antonova, Y. (2019). Пять лет буду тошнить всем назло [For five years I will be making all sick]. *Rbc.ru*. Retrieved from https://www.rbc.ru/politics/06/08/2019/5d42dbad9a7947887624fff0

Bikus, Z. (2019). World-low 9% of Ukrainians confident in government. *Gallup*. Retrieved from https://news.gallup.com/poll/247976/world-low-ukrainians-confident-government.aspx

Committee of Voters. (2020, May 15). За рік на державних посадах опинилися понад 30 «кварталівців» і їх знайомих [During the year, more than 30 members of "Kvartal 95" took public positions]. Retrieved from http://www.cvu.org.ua/nodes/view/type:news/slug:za-rik-na-derzhavnykh-posadakh-opynylysia-ponad-30-kvartalivtsiv-i-ikh-znaiomykh

Edwards, M. (2020, March 21). Ukraine's quiet depopulation crisis: The government is trying to entice its people back, not entirely successfully. *Atlantic*. Retrieved from https://www.theatlantic.com/international/archive/2020/03/ukraine-eastern-europe-depopulation-immigration-crisis/608464

Government Program. (2019, September 29). Програма діяльності Уряду [The program of government activities]. *Government Portal*. Retrieved from https://www.kmu.gov.ua/diyalnist/programa-diyalnosti-uryadu

IndustriAll. (2020, January 7). Draft labour law in Ukraine restricts union activities. *IndustriAll Global Union*. Retrieved from http://www.industriall-union.org/draft-labour-law-in-ukraine-restricts-union-activities

KIIS. (2019, October 14). Ставлення українців до політиків [Attitudes of Ukrainians to Politicians]. *Kyiv International Institute of Sociology*. Retrieved from http://kiis.com.ua/?lang=ukr&cat=reports&id=898&page=1

KIIS. (2020, February 24). Динаміка рейтингу підтримки політичних лідерів [Dynamics of the rating of support for political leaders and parties]. *Kyiv International Institute of Sociology*. Retrieved from https://www.kiis.com.ua/?lang=ukr&cat=reports&id=918&page=1

KIIS. (2021, August 2). Суспільно-політичні настрої населення України [Socio-political moods of Ukraine's population]. *Kyiv International Institute of Sociology*. Retrieved from http://kiis.com.ua/?lang=ukr&cat=reports&id=1055&page=1&fbclid=IwAR176knQ4Sj7Hppir8dxbKwpuWjo2Rnoky7O_5pvtU3DyY1UNJKgD_wxKgY

Laclau, E. (2005). *On populist reason*. New York: Verso.

Program. (n/d). Передвиборна програма партії "Слуга Народу" [The election platform of "Servant of the People" party]. *Servant of the People*. Retrieved from https://sluganarodu.com/program

Razumkov Center. (2019, October 11). Оцінка громадянами ситуації в країні [Citizens'assessment of the situation in the country]. Retrieved from http://razumkov.org.ua/napriamky/sotsiologichni-doslidzhennia/otsinka-gromadianamy-sytuatsii-v-kraini-ta-diialnosti-vlady-riven-doviry-do-sotsialnykh-instytutiv-ta-politykiv

RFE/RL. (2019, September 7). Ukraine's ratings upgraded by Fitch as debt declines, IMF deal likely. *Radio Free Europe/Radio Liberty*. Retrieved from https://www.rferl.org/a/ukraine-s-ratings-upgraded-by-fitch-as-debt-declines-imf-deal-likely/30151265.html

Servant of the People. (2015, November 18). Season 1, Episode 5. *YouTube*. Retrieved from https://www.youtube.com/watch?v=Yz3hsUi5qV4&list=PLkYIE2XK8v0Fbfr10H3VzzPj8OBaiB8ck&index=4

Servant of the People. (2016, June 2). Season 1, Episodes 1–4. *YouTube*. Retrieved from https://www.youtube.com/watch?v=_DXc_KyXdiU&t=790s

Servant of the People (2017a, October 25). Season 2, Episode 6. *YouTube*. Retrieved from https://www.youtube.com/watch?v=ADG9ZaRIokc

Servant of the People. (2017b, November 1). Season 2, Episode 14. *YouTube*. Retrieved from https://www.youtube.com/watch?v=b4vI7adzmEs

Servant of the People. (2017c, November 2). Season 2, Episode 16. *YouTube*. Retrieved from https://www.youtube.com/watch?v=JyIdyVH00P8.

Servant of the People. (2017d, November 8). Season 2, Episode 19. *YouTube.* Retrieved from https://www.youtube.com/watch?v=58vBVA8Wg_g&t=237s

Servant of the People (2019a, March 28). Season 3, Episode 1. *YouTube.* Retrieved from https://www.youtube.com/watch?v=BSjbZjAG5Tw

Servant of the People. (2019b, March 28). Season 3, Episode 2. *YouTube.* Retrieved from https://www.youtube.com/watch?v=pWAh0ViLorM

Servant of the People. (2019c, March 29). Season 3, Episode 3. *YouTube.* Retrieved from https://www.youtube.com/watch?v=iAFQGw8RM-g

UNIAN. (2019, September 6). Рамочка турборежима [A turbo mode frame]. Retrieved from https://www.unian.net/politics/10675335-ramochka-turborezhima-v-sluge-naroda-planiruyut-prinimat-ne-menee-7-10-zakonoproektov-za-den.html

Zelensky, V. (2019a, May 20). Інавгураційна промова [Inaugural address]. *President of Ukraine Official Website.* Retrieved from https://www.president.gov.ua/news/inavguracijna-promova-prezidenta-ukrayini-volodimira-zelensk-55489

Zelensky, V. (2019b, September 2). Зустріч Зеленського з керівництвом ВРУ, Кабміну та правоохоронних органів [Zelensky's meeting with the leadership of the Verkhovna Rada, the Cabinet of Ministers and law enforcement agencies]. *YouTube.* Retrieved from https://www.youtube.com/watch?v=76n6VhC3p8A

Zelensky, V. (2019c, September 30). Зеленский: Кривой Рог моего детства — это бандитский город 90-х [Zelensky: Kryvyi Rih of my childhood is a gangster city of the 90s]. *YouTube.* Retrieved from https://www.youtube.com/watch?v=P8nMfcoWCrM

Zelensky, V. (2019d, October 10). Пресс-марафон Зеленского [The press marathon of Zelensky]. *YouTube.* Retrieved from https://www.youtube.com/watch?v=Bymos8VMVqk

Zelensky, V. (2019e, November 7). Zelensky in Tesla. *YouTube.* Retrieved from https://www.youtube.com/watch?v=oyUqwB8bBGE

Zelensky, V. (2020, March 30). Внеочередное заседание Рады [An extraordinary meeting of the Verkhovna Rada]. *YouTube.* Retrieved from https://www.youtube.com/watch?v=k0HKrHnsYgM

Zelensky, V. (2021, August 5). Самое главное для жителей оккупированных территорий понять: Родина или ты гость? [The most important thing for residents of the occupied territories is to understand: Homeland or are you a guest?] YouTube. Retrieved from https://www.youtube.com/watch?v=tEdgF1v2Rwo

4 On the Fringes of the Virtual and the Real

Simulating the Political

The Virtual-Real Election Platform

The case of Zelensky is a complex interrelation of the discursive and the material, with the former and the latter existing in both digital and non-digital realms. In analyzing it, I have considered the discursive-material knot in both planes—"the virtual" and "the real"—as well as their interrelations. Following the logic of Deleuze and Guattari (1988, see Chapter 2), I traced the formation of Zelensky's political assemblage, which encompasses both digital and non-digital realms. I also traced the formation of the equivalential chain of election promises made by Zelensky-Holoborodko across the "interface" that separates "the virtual" from "the real." To proceed with this kind of analysis, I drew on Laclau's method of analyzing populist discourses (2005), developed from DT's foundations (Chapter 2). While doing my research, I took "Zelensky" (the discursive-material assemblage of his name and body) as an empty signifier, linked equivalentially both to Zelensky's election promises made in "real" life and Holoborodko's fulfilling of them in the digital/virtual realm of the series.

One may object that Holoborodko's actions in the show have nothing to do with Zelensky's promises during his "real" election campaign, but the point is that in "reality," Zelensky "had spent little time articulating how, exactly, he was planning to execute his proposed reforms," as Joshua Yaffa (2019) noted. His pre-election speeches and interviews were so infrequent they could be counted on one's fingers. The only way the people of Ukraine could get an idea of how Zelensky was planning to fix the country's many problems was by watching his show. After all, he was not only an actor, but also the co-owner of the studio producing it and co-author of the scripts, and for many observers it was quite clear before the election that voters would take Holoborodko's

DOI: 10.4324/9781003228493-5

promises as Zelensky's. The following is an excerpt from one of his rare pre-election interviews in which the issue is addressed:

HOST: But do you understand that millions of viewers who will watch your show will associate you with Vasiliy Petrovich Holoborodko[1] and will be voting not so much for you as for him?

[Но понимаешь ли ты, что миллионы зрителей, которые посмотрят эти фильмы—три фильма больших—будут отождествлять тебя с Василием Петровичем Голобородько и будут голосовать не так за тебя, как за него?]

ZELENSKY: I didn't invent all this [the show]—I felt all this, I am really feeling this… It would have been impossible to create it all simply because I am a good actor and because someone wrote it well. We wrote it together, we all lived it together.

[Все это не выдумано—я все это прочувствовал. Я реально это чувствую. Это все нельзя было создать просто потому, что я хороший актер и кто-то хорошо это написал. Мы все это написали вместе, мы все это прожили].

(Zelensky, 2018, 6:28–7:47)

Zelensky's answer is not straightforward, but its meaning is clear. By arguing that the show was not simply a piece of artistic creation but made from his real feelings, Zelensky established unequivocal links between his "real" self and his "virtual" double Holoborodko, implying that they were essentially the same.

Zelensky's election platform started with the phrase: "I will tell you about the Ukraine of my dream" [Я розповім Вам про Україну своєї мрії] (Zelensky, 2019a). In what followed, he linked this dream to such master-signifiers as "peace" [мир], "people's rule" [народовладдя], "human dignity" [людська гідність], "equality" [рівність], "justice" [справедливість], and "prosperity" [заможність]. In the economic sphere, all these signifiers were equivalentially united with: "de-shadowing the economy" [детінізація економіки], "full governmental transparency" [повна відкритість діяльності влади], and "victory over corruption" [перемога над корупцією].

Consisting of only 1,601 words, the platform did not provide details as to how "de-shadowing the economy," "victory over corruption," "equality," and "justice" could be achieved. Zelensky's few interviews and speeches in "real life" were also "light on policy specifics," as Yaffa (2019) put it. All the nodal points of the platform would have remained completely empty if they had not been linked to the actions of "digital" Holoborodko. Only through his "virtual" anti-corruption performance did the empty signifiers of Zelensky's "real" position acquire meaning. In other words, Zelensky's "dream" came to be filled with meanings through being equivalentially united not only with the discursive elements of his platform, speeches, and interviews but also with the virtual performance of Holoborodko in the realm of the digital.

Zelensky's election pledges were given to Ukrainians in "real" life; however, it is in the digital realm of the series that Zelensky-Holoborodko demonstrated how these pledges could be implemented. In other words, by means of Holoborodko—his virtual double—Zelensky was able to deliver his election promises not in terms of just telling, but performing. In the show, Holoborodko unites the split country, fires dishonest government officials, imprisons corrupted politicians, and shows by his own example what the "servants of the people"—political elites—should be. Season by season, for three years in a row, Zelensky-Holoborodko was showing the people of Ukraine what should be done to pull the country out of the swamp of corruption, poverty, mutual animosity, and hopelessness. He was able to do so by transforming the "real" into the "digital" and vice versa.

Zelensky's political success cannot be explained without accounting for his play "through the interface" that separates "the virtual" and "the real." By the logic of invitation and dislocation (Carpentier, 2017, 2021), the digital materiality of the series participated in discursive struggles characterizing the Ukrainian political field. An event of its own, *Servant of the People* dislocated the normality of the hegemonic political discourse according to which only professional politicians and rich people could win presidential elections, with their top priority in ruling the country being their own personal benefit. The story of Holoborodko-the-teacher—a poor, honest simpleton with a better understanding of history than contemporary political life—unequivocally invited viewers to imagine an alternative was possible: Not only could common people, with no wealth or power, win the popular vote, but they could also use political power to serve the people rather than their own interests.

Interacting with Zelensky's virtual-real creation, sympathetic viewers were interpellated into Zelensky's performative machine, which disrupted the conventional flow of political business. The invitation extended to Ukrainians by the series—to dream about and act in the name of another Ukraine, ruled not by professional-and-corrupted politicians but by unprofessional-but-honest people—was accepted by millions; the number of votes cast in favor of Zelensky in April 2019 clearly testifies to this. On May 30, 2019, the collective fantasy generated by Zelensky's dream machine materialized into the discursive-material assemblage of the presidential mace in Zelensky's right hand and presidential collar around his neck—the symbols of Ukraine's highest political power. His oath of allegiance to the Ukrainian people with his right hand on the Bible; his first speech in the capacity of the President of Ukraine; his announcement of the dissolution of the parliament during the inauguration—to a great extent, these discursive-material manifestations of presidential power were made possible by the *Servant of the People* machine crushing up all frontiers between the imagined and the real, the artistic and the political, the digital and the tangible, and so forth.

Clearly, not all Ukrainians accepted the show's invitation to disrupt the hegemonic political order and transfer presidential power to an amateur. Many critics of Zelensky invested his performance on the fringes of the virtual and the real with the meaning of "clown tricks": "Why is it so funny to all of us? Because our president is a clown" [Чому нам смішно? Тому що в нас президент клоун] (Chornovol, 2020, 0:27–0:29). Such was an alternative reaction to Zelensky's project widely shared by his opponents. The possibility of interpreting the whole situation in these terms was offered by the obvious fact that the "real" Zelensky was not the "virtual" simpleton Holoborodko—the "real" Zelensky was a well-known and well-to-do comedian, and this only added to the contingency of the whole discursive-material situation and the possibility of interpreting it in different ways.

The "presidential activities" performed by Holoborodko in the series were so cinematically simplistic and they could only strengthen the "clown tricks" discourse. In the show, oligarchs buy their way out of criminal cases to cover the state budget deficit, while ordinary Ukrainians donate money to pay off IMF debts. On the other hand, those who were inclined to support Zelensky while recognizing the extreme naivety of the show's presentation of "reforms" were free to adopt a "this is just a show" position. The contingency of the whole virtual-real discursive-material assemblage provided Ukrainians with an opportunity to identify themselves with it in different ways, which demonstrates not only the agency of the viewers/Ukrainian citizens but also the agency of the show itself. By triggering different reactions among Ukrainians, the show itself acted as a social agent. Once the series had been released, the producers could not control its impact.[2]

Obviously, Zelensky's success cannot be explained exclusively by the series. Zelensky's victory became possible due to many different factors, the most important of which was the ongoing war in Donbas along with the deterioration of socioeconomic conditions. As pointed out by Vadim Karasyov, director of the Kyiv-based Institute for Global

Strategies, Poroshenko's crushing defeat in the presidential election of April 2019 came as a result of people's fatigue with the "paranoid politics" [параноидальной политики] of fear associated with the conflict, when "every day here is an agent of Moscow, an agent of the Kremlin, an agent of Russia, an agent of the FBI…" [Когда каждый день тот агент Москвы, тот агент Кремля, тот агент России, тот агент ФСБ] (Karasyov, 2019, 15:00–15:06). According to Karasyov, corrupted elites "switched paranoia on" [включать паранойю] to hold on to political power, while people wanted "to return to normal life and get out of this madhouse" [вернуться к нормальной жизни и выбраться из этого дурдома]. Political decisions were thus driven by a widely shared request for peace, national unity, and centrism (Karasyov, 2019, 16:20–18:50). In their desire for "the normal," the majority of Ukrainians voted for the alternative proposed by Zelensky: a beautiful, bright, humorous dream in which peace reigns and there is no splitting of the country into "right" and "wrong" Ukrainians.

However, the recognition of other factors contributing to Zelensky's success does not diminish the importance of his series, in which the most painful issues of "real" Ukraine were transformed into bits to be solved performatively in the realm of the digital. In this sense, Zelensky used the series as a virtual-real political program—"a very cool move, because no one reads boring texts now" [Это очень классный ход. Потому что нудные тексты сейчас никто не читает] (Karasyov, 2019, 11:13–11:18). It was "virtual" in the sense that it was presented through a fictional character living in the "intangible" digital world, but it was "real" because it influenced political developments on the ground by convincing people (not all, but many) that simplistic, Holoborodko-style political solutions could actually improve the situation in Ukraine. This finding is in line with Paul Leonardi (2010) who argues that, apart from its molecular/radical/vital materiality, digital reality is perfectly material in the sense that it leads to practical social consequences.

Zelensky's Party Machine

The presentation of the social with a Manichean division between "good us" and "bad them" culminates in the second season of the show when Holoborodko-the-president, having lost faith in the possibility of anti-corruption reforms within the existing system of power, unleashes his fury with machine guns, slaughtering the parliamentary deputies right in the session hall of the parliamentary building. Moments after the shooting scene, it becomes clear that this is Holoborodko's dream, not "reality," even in the show. However, as it turned out, not all people saw the shooting as a mere fantasy.

On April 12, 2019, the First Deputy Chair of Ukraine's parliament, Irina Herashchenko, demanded that the Ministry of Internal Affairs open criminal proceedings in connection with the parliament shooting scene in *Servant of the People* (Interfax, 2019). She interpreted the scene as "the language of hatred" [язык вражды]. Anton Herashchenko, a representative of the Ministry of Internal Affairs, responded: It was in dreams; dreams can be different, but one cannot punish for dreams—dreams are not punishable [Это было в мечтах, во сне, а сны могут быть разными, но за сны не наказывают—сны не наказуемы] (НВ Ukraine, 2019).

If the shooting of the parliament was an allegorical expression of Zelensky's dream to get rid of the old system of power, whose corruption *Servant of the People* had been revealing for three TV seasons in a row, then the time had come to make those dreams true: "I dissolve the Verkhovna Rada of the eighth convocation. Glory to Ukraine!" [Я розпускаю Верховну Раду України 8-го скликання. Слава Україні!] (Zelensky, 2019b). For many, these words, pronounced by Zelensky at his actual inauguration, were the equivalent of Holoborodko's imagined shooting. "Do you remember, there was an episode where he was shooting the parliament? Now, he has shot the parliament by words" [Помните, есть такой эпизод, где он расстреливает парламент? А вот сейчас он его расстрелял, этот парламент, словесно]—said Karasyov following Zelensky's announcement (Gamov, 2019), which got a standing ovation from his viewers/voters watching the inauguration ceremony in front of the parliamentary building.

Two months after Zelensky's inauguration, his *Servant of the People* party received the majority of parliamentary seats. No one could predict such an overwhelming success given that the party members were predominantly unknown to the general public before the elections. The consensus view among many political experts is that Ukrainians seemed to cast their votes for unknown "new faces" simply because they were running under the brand of the party with the show's name and because people were tired of the "old faces" of the corrupted establishment (e.g., Skorkin, 2019).

Never in its history had the parliament of Ukraine welcomed so many politically inexperienced "people's servants." To provide them with at least some basic knowledge of their parliamentary duties, the party organized an intense training course in a hotel complex in the

Carpathian foothills. Mykyta Poturaev, a party ideologist,[3] addressed his colleagues in this way:

> Politically, you are nothing…You are here because the voter was looking for people from the political party "Servant of the People." The voter did not care whose name would be on that line. The winner of these elections is Vladimir Alexandrovich Zelensky.
>
> [Все вы—политически никто… Как вы здесь оказались? Вы здесь оказались потому, что избиратель искал людей политической партии "Слуга народа". И ему было все равно, какая фамилия будет указана в этой строке. Эти выборы выиграл Владимир Александрович Зеленский].
>
> (Poturaev, 2019)

Shocking as it may sound, this statement makes sense from the point of view of democratic representation. One can hardly regard the "servants" as representatives of voters who simply did not know them and had never heard their political views. Among the elected political newbies were wedding photographers, actors, and nannies with no political experience whatsoever (Lenta.ru, 2019).

Bewildering observers yet again, all the "key people" of the party wrote their letters of resignation in advance. As Zelensky himself commented on the issue,

> We do not hold on to power. We—all the key people who came with me—agreed from the beginning that we would write letters of resignation. If society or the president feels that this or that person cannot cope with the tasks set by Ukraine, then this person will resign any moment.
>
> [Ми не тримаємося за владу. Ми—всі ключові люди, які зі мною прийшли—домовилися з самого початку, що напишемо заяви на звільнення. Якщо суспільство чи президент відчуватимуть, що та чи інша людина не може впоратися з поставленими Україною завданнями, то в будь-який момент ця людина, не тримаючись за крісло, піде у відставку].
>
> (Radio Liberty, 2019)

One could get an impression that the idea of these letters was to prevent "servants" from using their political power for personal financial gain. As it turned out later, however, "coping with the tasks set by Ukraine" meant adopting unpopular laws necessary for the country's neoliberal "normalization." In a video clip released in November 2019, Zelensky pronounced:

> Every deputy must understand that he or she must vote for the laws that society needs. Not all bills are popular. No wonder they have not been adopted for 30 years.

> [Кожен депутат повинен зрозуміти, що він повинен голосувати за закони, які потрібні суспільству. Не всі законопроекти популярні. Не просто так же їх не приймали народні депутати впродовж 30 років].

(Zelensky, 2019c, 3:54–4:09)

Zelensky's proposed methods for controlling the "servants" had significant potential to hamper the political process by silencing alternative opinions and stifling the possibility of internal dissent. Prerequisites came into force through which an "authoritarian neoliberalism" (Bruff, 2014) could emerge from ostensibly democratic procedures—even more of an empty simulation of democracy than the simulacrum ridiculed by Zelensky in the show (more on this in Chapter 8). Zelensky himself seems to acknowledge this. "We have democracy in the Verkhovna Rada so far. But only so far…" [Поки що у нас демократія у Верховній Раді. Але поки що] (Zelensky, 2019c, 0:28–0:32)—this is how, with a meaningful grin on his face, Zelensky commented on the necessity of voting for the "laws society needs."

As Karasyov put it as soon as the *Servant of the People* faction achieved a parliamentary majority,

> There will be a parliament of obedient people, it will be a prison of deputies… because they were not elected, they were actually appointed… There will be iron discipline, an iron cage for deputies, they will vote as either the Cabinet or the Presidential Office decides.

> [Сейчас парламент не нужен, сейчас будет парламент послушных людей, это будет тюрьма депутатов… потому что их не избрали, их назначили фактически… Там будет железная дисциплина, железная клетка для депутатов, они будут голосовать так, как решит либо Кабмин, либо Офис президента].[4]

(Gladkov, 2019)

It seemed like the deputies had been cast for parliamentary roles similar to those of their fictional counterparts on the TV program, in which Holoborodko also hires and fires people without regard to legality. Right after his electoral victory, as if still playing the part of Holoborodko, Zelensky traveled all over Ukraine to wallop local bureaucrats for the pleasure of viewers—not of the series this time, but of news programs. Amid such developments, the imaginary and the real have merged into a virtual game where every player is at the mercy of a system that holds a monopoly over the rules—a despotism for virtual times, as Baudrillard (2005) would call this (more on this in Chapter 7).

To put it in Slobodian's (2020) terms, it appears as if Zelensky's power machine was designed exclusively for "finding a legal and institutional fix for the disruptive effects of democracy on market processes" (p. 11). By trying to control parliamentary deputies through unprecedented disciplinary mechanisms, Zelensky was clearly attempting to de-politicize his neoliberal economic policy (see Chapter 8). To be sure, Zelensky's case in this sense is far from unique—"the disenchantment of politics by economics" (Davies, 2017, p. xx) seems to be a common feature of otherwise different neoliberal projects. However, Zelensky's contribution to the general trend is radically innovative: Not only was his project of neoliberalization not-so-political, it also appeared to be not-so-real. The condition of possibility for Zelensky's neoliberal project was the creation of a zone of exception where the virtual and the real were not mutually exclusive but rather blurred into one another. In this respect, Zelensky surpassed even his "great teacher"—as he called Donald Trump during phone talks with the then-US president (CNN, 2019). Both were showmen and each of them boasted he was "not a politician" (Trump, 2016; RFE/RL, 2019); however, Trump was making election promises as himself, while Zelensky did it predominantly as the TV character Holoborodko.

Holoborodko-Zelensky-Holoborodko

In line with Fraser's (2019) argument, for Zelensky's neoliberal project to gain broader appeal, it had to be repackaged—decked out as progressive. In other words, it had to be euphemized through articulating linkages not with mass privatization, budget cuts, land sales, and so forth, but with concepts like civil peace, social justice, Europeanization, modernization, and normalization. The second chain replaced the first one, which had come to be totally invisible in Holoborodko's presentation. In Zelensky's show, so popular among Ukrainians, Holoborodko does not privatize public enterprises and land. In contrast, he promises "to expropriate the property of state officials by the same methods that they acquired it in the 1990s" [Мы забираем имущество теми методами, которыми они это имущество в 90-х приобрели] (*Servant of the People*, 2017b, 19:26–19:31). This formulation suggested that the bandit post-Soviet privatization of the 1990s should be reconsidered and social justice restored through returning to the state people's once-collective property. However, instead of the nationalization of the property once stolen from the people, Zelensky declared another round of privatization as soon as his real Cabinet of ministers was formed.

Only after his popular support plummeted in 2021 did Zelensky return to the rhetoric of re-privatization to save his approval rating. On February 20, 2021, the Secretary of the National Security and Defense Council (NSDC) Oleksiy Danilov announced the beginning of re-privatization through sanctions. Strictly in line with Holoborodko's message regarding the expropriation of collective property by the same methods oligarchs received it in the 1990s (see Chapter 3), Danilov proclaimed: "Everything that has been stolen from the Ukrainian people since 1991 will be returned to the Ukrainian people" [Все, что украдено с 1991 года у украинского народа, будет возвращено украинскому народу] (Strana.ua, 2021).

Furthermore, as in the show, the return of public property to the people was planned to be conducted without regard to legality. As Mikhail Pogrebinsky (2021), director of the Kyiv Centre of Political Studies and Conflictology, explains,

> The decisions of the National Security and Defense Council—put into effect by presidential decrees—imposed sanctions against a number of Ukrainian individuals and legal entities. It was done ignoring the direct constitutional prohibition to impose sanctions against Ukrainian citizens. These sanctions involve the extrajudicial seizure of property without any evidence of illegal activities of the relevant individuals and legal entities.

Considered alongside the governmental program of mass privatization, which Zelensky said in March 2021 would go on no matter what (Economic Pravda, 2021), his desire to nationalize the property of sanctioned Ukrainian citizens looks to many like political reprisal rather than a righting of past injustice.

Among the first to be sanctioned by the NSDC were two parliamentary deputies from the Opposition Platform "For Life" (OPZZh)—Victor Medvedchuk and Taras Kozak, as well as members of their families.[5] Three oppositional television channels controlled by these politicians were shut down (Olearchuk, 2021). Reporters Without Borders considered this "an abuse of the government's power to impose sanctions that could lead to an increase in partisan tension" and demanded that Ukraine "respect its international obligations" (RSF, 2021); the channels have remained banned, however, allowing Zelensky to make some political headway:

> In recent months, the OPZZh has been gaining in polls at the expense of the president's Servant of the People party, and after the Council took its most recent decisions, polls have shown an increase of several percent in support for Zelensky and his party.
>
> (Matuszak & Żochowski, 2021)

At least partly, Zelensky's bump in popularity after attacking the opposition can be explained by the fact that, in contrast to the land reform and other neoliberal experiments launched by "servants," people generally liked the idea of punishing oligarchs or simply rich influential people (oppositional or not) by all possible means (legal or not).[6]

Inspired by this success, Zelensky started using the NSDC to apply sanctions—extrajudicially and on a grand scale—against other citizens of Ukraine suspected of various crimes. In June 2021 alone, Zelensky put into effect a NSDC decision to impose sanctions against 538 individuals and 540 companies (Ukrayinska Pravda, 2021). Despite independent observers having significant doubts "about the use of the broadly and vaguely formulated concept of a 'threat to national security' to resolve the current internal problems related to the management of the state in the economic, political and administrative spheres," the show of illegal sanctions, politically profitable for Zelensky, still goes on. As Pogrebinsky (2021) put it, "We are witnessing the establishment of a pro-Western authoritarian regime in Ukraine, where power is concentrated in the hands of the president." It is difficult not to agree with this observation.[7]

Indeed, as we can judge from both Zelensky's election platform and his show, the power of the presidency had to be strengthened to implement reforms aimed at achieving a "normal" Westernized condition. In the series, Westernization (modernization) was equivalentially united with social justice, understood as de-oligarchization, re-privatization, and the fair distribution of national resources; but in real life, during the first period of Zelensky's rule (2019–2020), Westernization was linked primarily to the neoliberal reforms discussed in the previous chapter. Only in 2021, with an approval rating in freefall, did Zelensky invoke Holoborodko's ideas of restoring social justice through re-privatization and de-oligarchization and initiate the NSDC's out-of-court proceedings.

A similar revival of Holoborodko's promises can be observed with regard to other issues, such as the relationship between Ukraine and the IMF. In the show, the virtual president Holoborodko publicly curses the IMF after the director of its mission withholds a new loan, setting humiliating terms that could destroy the economy of Ukraine: "With a deep sense of gratitude, I would like to tell you: 'Fuck off!'" [С чувством глубокой благодарности хочу сказать: "Идите в жопу!"] (*Servant of the People*, 2017a, 22:59–23:03). In reality, the government of Zelensky is still negotiating with the IMF, asking for new loans and adding to the country's already-mountainous level of debt:

> Ukraine's public and publicly guaranteed debt increased from 50.4 percent of GDP in 2019 to a projected 65.4 percent in 2020, according to the IMF. In December alone, Ukraine's Finance Ministry raised roughly $4 billion in government bonds, with the majority of the securities at interest rates between 10–12 percent. Among other debt, Ukraine also announced a $350 million short-term loan from Deutsche Bank that month. According to Ukraine's finance ministry, the country will have to repay roughly $11 billion during the first half of 2021, or about 7 percent of the country's GDP. It will then have to repay roughly an additional $10 billion during the rest of 2021.
>
> (Timtchenko, 2021)

However, with regard to the IMF—as in the earlier case of re-privatization—a stance championed by Holoborodko in the virtual realm later reappeared on Zelensky's public agenda in 2021 to shore up his approval rating. In his joint interview with *Agence France-Presse*, *Reuters*, and *the Associated Press* on June 14, 2021, Zelensky accused the IMF of "unfair" policies toward Ukraine; in his view, IMF requirements should be mitigated given that "we have a war," "we are fighting the oligarchs," and "we are fighting corruption" (Zelensky, 2021). Of course, accusing the IMF of unfairness is not the same as cussing out its representatives, but what is important is that Holoborodko's "virtual" themes are reemerging in Zelensky's "real" discursive constructions when it becomes tactically necessary.

It is important to recognize, in other words, that Zelensky's power, which has been formed on the fringes of the virtual and the real, still draws its energy from the virtual realm—from the promises of Holoborodko and from the party machine that, as I will discuss in Chapter

7, has become the virtual reality of his show—"an ectoplasm of the screen," in the words of Baudrillard (2005, p. 81). In the next two chapters, using the example of land reform, I will discuss how exactly this machine, refueled with virtual energy, has managed to function despite people's disapproval.

Notes

1 "Vasiliy Petrovich" is a Russian equivalent for "Vasyl Petrovych."
2 After the episodes of Servant of the People aired on 1+1 television channel, they were uploaded to YouTube and any viewer has been able to watch any episode free of charge.
3 Poturaev is a political technologist with a long service record, having worked for numerous well-known politicians including Ukraine's ex-president Leonid Kuchma. Since 2019, he has been an influential force in Zelensky's political project (Ukraina.ru, 2019).
4 In 2020, amid Zelensky's flagging popularity, the parliamentary "mono-majority" of his party started fragmenting into informal groups influenced by oligarchs. To get bills approved, "servants" now have to negotiate with "dissidents."
5 The sanctions against Victor Medvedchuk and Taras Kozak were imposed under the premise of investigating their alleged involvement in "financing terrorism"—i.e., having economic relations with Donbas. Because Donbas rebels are considered "terrorists" (Baysha, 2017), it is implied that the Donbas and Luhansk republics, which had announced their independence from Ukraine, are also terroristic organizations. Any economic relations with them may therefore be interpreted as support for terrorism. Sanctions ban the use and management of property; restrict trade operations; block the transit of resources, flights and shipments across Ukraine; prohibit the withdrawal of capital from Ukraine; suspend economic and financial obligations due to the sanctioned party; stop the issuing of permissions and licenses on the import and export of currency; and restrict cash withdrawals from cards discharged by foreign residents (Hurska, 2021).
6 Medvedchuk, a sanctioned OPZZh deputy and strident opponent of Zelensky who systematically criticized the reforms carried out by the "servants," is a millionaire who accumulated his initial capital in the 1990s. The godfather of Medvedchuk's daughter is none other than Vladimir Putin—another fact that may make Medvedchuk loathsome in the eyes of many West-looking Ukrainians. However, he improvement of Zelensky's rating was short-lived: In August 2021, the gap in approval ratings between OPZZh (18.3 percent) and Servant of the People (20.6 percent) fell within the statistical margin of error of the polling, while disapproval of Zelensky rose to 56.1 percent (up from 52.7 percent in July [KIIS, 2021]).
7 Zelensky's drive to impose sanctions on Ukrainian citizens went beyond a single instance of violating the Constitution. After the Constitutional Court of Ukraine ruled the powers of the National Agency of Preventing Corruption (NAPC) unconstitutional and scrapped the asset declaration system—a program that had been one of the requirements for Ukraine's loans from the IMF—Zelensky drafted a law to fire all the Court's sitting judges and

annul their ruling. Experts agreed that the bill was "clearly in violation of the Ukrainian Constitution, which only allows Constitutional Court judges to be removed by a vote of two-thirds of their colleagues" (Harvard, n/d). The head of Ukraine's Constitutional Court, Oleksandr Tupytskyi, called Zelensky's move a "coup"—exactly as Zelensky had described similar actions taken by Holoborodko in the show. In response to Tupytskyi's remark, on March 27, 2021—also in violation of the Ukrainian Constitution—Zelensky signed a decree canceling his appointment as a judge of the court.

References

Baudrillard, J. (2005). *The intelligence of evil*. New York: Berg.

Baysha, O. (2017). In the name of national security: Articulating ethno-political struggles as terrorism. *Journal of Multicultural Discourses, 12*(4), 332–348. doi: 10.1080/17447143.2017.1363217

Bruff, I. (2014). The rise of authoritarian neoliberalism. *Rethinking Marxism, 26*(1), 113–129.

Carpentier, N. (2017). *The discursive-material knot: Cyprus in conflict and community media participation*. New York: Peter Lang.

Carpentier, N. (2021). Doing justice to the agential material: A reflection on a non-hierarchical repositioning of the discursive and the material. *Journal of Language and Politics, 20*(1), 112–128. https://doi.org/10.1075/jlp.20045.car

Chornovol, T. (2020). We are not laughing because our president is a clown. *YouTube*. Retrieved from https://www.youtube.com/watch?v=e4gSEoC6CYU

CNN. (2019, September 26). Telephone conversation with President Zelenskyy of Ukraine. Retrieved from https://www.cnn.com/2019/09/25/politics/donald-trump-ukraine-transcript-call/index.html

Davies, W. (2017. *The limits of neoliberalism: Authority, sovereignty and the logic of competition*. London: Sage.

Deleuze, G., & Guattari, F. (1988). *A thousand plateaus. Capitalism and schizophrenia*. London: Athlone Press.

Economic Pravda. (2021, March 18). Зеленский заявил, что процесс приватизации продолжится [Zelensky said the privatization process will continue]. Retrieved from https://www.epravda.com.ua/rus/news/2021/03/18/672087

Fraser, N. (2019). *The old is dying and the new cannot be born: From progressive neoliberalism to Trump and Beyond*. New York: Verso.

Gamov, A. (2019, May 20). Теперь начнётся война нового Зеленского со старым Парламентом [Now, the war between the new Zelensky and the old parliament will start]. *Komsomolskaya Pravda*. Retrieved from https://www.kp.ru/daily/26978/4037511/

Gladkov, V. (2019, July 24). Карасёв рассказал, кто пришёл на смену кошкам и котам в Верховной Раде [Karasyov told who had replaced cats in the Verkhovna Rada]. *Politnavigator*. Retrieved from https://www.politnavigator.news/karasjov-rasskazal-kto-prishjol-na-smenu-koshkam-i-kotam-v-verkhovnojj-rade.html

Harvard. (n/d). Ukraine's constitutional court crisis, explained. *Ukrainian Research Institute Harvard University*. Retrieved from https://huri.harvard.edu/ukraine-constitutional-court-crisis-explained

HB Ukraine. (2019). Сериал "Слуга народа" должен быть настольной книгой политиков [The series "Servant of the People" should be a handbook for politicians]. Retrieved from https://nv.ua/ukraine/politics/anton-gerashchenko-serial-sluga-naroda-dolzhen-byt-nastolnoy-knigoy-politikov-50017134.html

Hurska, A. (2021, February 24). Ukraine's sanctions against pro-Russian oligarch Medvedchuk. *Eurasia Daily Monitor*. Retrieved from https://jamestown.org/program/ukraines-sanctions-against-pro-russian-oligarch-medvedchuk-all-about-oil-and-coal/

Interfax. (2019, April 12). И. Геращенко просит МВД возбудить дело против авторов "Слуги Народа" [I. Heraschenko asks the Ministry of Internal Affairs to open a case against "Servant of the People's" authors]. Retrieved from https://interfax.com.ua/news/election2019/580248.html

Karasyov, V. (2019, April 10). Вадим Карасев на 112 [Vadim Karasyov na 112]. *YouTube*. Retrieved from https://www.youtube.com/watch?v=L6g443XgNPw

KIIS. (2021, August 2). Суспільно-політичні настрої населення України [Socio-political moods of Ukraine's population]. Retrieved from http://kiis.com.ua/?lang=ukr&cat=reports&id=1055&page=1&fbclid=IwAR176knQ4Sj7Hppir8dxbKwpuWjo2Rnoky7O_5pvtU3DyY1UNJKgD_wxKgY

Lenta.ru. (2019, July 22). Свадебный фотограф из партии Зеленского [Zelenskiy's party wedding photographer]. Retrieved from https://lenta.ru/news/2019/07/22/narphotograf/

Leonardi, P. M. (2010). Digital materiality? How artifacts without matter, matter. *First Monday, 15*(6), 1–20. doi: 10.5210/fm.v15i6.3036

Matuszak, S., & Żochowski, P. (2021, April 1). Growing importance of the Security Council in Ukraine. *Center for Eastern Studies*. Retrieved from https://www.osw.waw.pl/en/publikacje/analyses/2021-04-01/growing-importance-security-council-ukraine

Olearchuk, R. (2021, February 3). Ukraine shuts TV channels it accuses of spreading "Russian Disinformation." *Financial Times*. Retrieved from https://www.ft.com/content/176c0332-b927-465d-9eac-3b2d7eb9706a

Pogrebinsky, M. (2021, April 6). Why Zelensky's Ukraine is becoming increasingly autocratic. *National Interest*. Retrieved from https://nationalinterest.org/feature/why-zelensky%E2%80%99s-ukraine-becoming-increasingly-autocratic-182124

Poturaev, M. (2019, July 30). "Вы—никто." Лекция Потураева перед «слугами народа» в Трускавце ["You are nobody." Poturayev's lecture to "servants of the people" in Truskavets | *YouTube*, Retrieved from https://www.youtube.com/watch?v=ctcxD1hcah8

Radio Liberty. (2019, August 2). Zelensky confirmed that Boghdan has written a letter of resignation. Retrieved from https://www.radiosvoboda.org/a/news-bohdan-vidstavka/30088799.html

RFE/RL. (2019, April 21). Poroshenko faces tough test as Ukraine votes in presidential runoff. *Radio Free Europe/Radio Liberty*. Retrieved from https://www.rferl.org/a/poroshenko-faces-zelenskiy-second-round-ukraine-presidential-vote/29893693.html

RSF. (2021, February 26). Ukraine escalates "information war" by banning three pro-Kremlin media. *Reporters Without Borders*. Retrieved from https://rsf.org/en/news/ukraine-escalates-information-war-banning-three-pro-kremlin-media

Servant of the People. (2017a, November 1). Season 2, Episode 14. *YouTube*. Retrieved from https://www.youtube.com/watch?v=b4vI7adzmEs

Servant of the People. (2017b, November 2). Season 2, Episode 16. *YouTube*. Retrieved from https://www.youtube.com/watch?v=JyIdyVH00P8

Skorkin, K. (2019, July 23). Карт-бланш для «слуги народа» [Carte blanche for the "servant of the people"]. *Forbes*. Retrieved from https://www.forbes.ru/obshchestvo/380623-kartblansh-dlya-slugi-naroda-kak-zelenskiy-realizoval-v-zhizni-scenariy-iz

Slobodian, Q. (2020). *Globalists: The end of empire and the birth of neoliberalism*. Cambridge, MA: Harvard University Press.

Strana.ua. (2021, February 20). Данилов анонсировал начало реприватизации в Украине [Danilov announced the start of reprivatization in Ukraine]. Retrieved from https://strana.ua/news/318762-danilov-rasskazal-protiv-koho-snbo-planiruet-vvodit-sanktsii.html

Timtchenko, I. (2021, February 26). Ukraine's debt problem spells trouble. *Foreign Policy*. Retrieved from https://foreignpolicy.com/2021/02/26/imf-review-ukraine-debt-gdp-linked-warrants-reform

Trump (2016, August 21). I am not a politician, thank goodness. *YouTube*. Retrieved from https://www.youtube.com/watch?v=JyRCzxUACrg

Ukraina.ru. (2019, November 19). Никита Потураев: кто он? [Mykyta Poturaev: Who is he?]. Retrieved from https://ukraina.ru/news/20191119/1025720994.html

Ukrayinska Pravda. (2021, June 24). Зеленский ввел санкции против Фукса, Фирташа и окружения Путина [Zelensky imposed sanctions against Fuchs, Firtash and entourage Putin]. Retrieved from https://www.pravda.com.ua/rus/news/2021/06/24/7298344/

Yaffa, J. (2019, October 25). Ukraine's unlikely president, promising a new style of politics, gets a taste of Trump's swamp. *New Yorker*. Retrieved from https://www.newyorker.com/magazine/2019/11/04/how-trumps-emissaries-put-pressure-on-ukraines-new-president

Zelensky, V. (2018, December 25). В гостях у Дмитрия Гордона [Visiting Dmytro Gordon]. *YouTube*. Retrieved from https://www.youtube.com/watch?v=VPE2hv8qbBc

Zelensky, V. (2019a, n/d). Передвиборча програма кандидата на пост Президента України Володимира Зеленського [Election program of the candidate for President of Ukraine Volodymyr Zelensky]. Retrieved from https://program.ze2019.com/

Zelensky, V. (2019b, May 20). Інавгураційна промова [Inaugural address]. *President of Ukraine Official Website.* Retrieved from https://www.president. gov.ua/news/inavguracijna-promova-prezidenta-ukrayini-volodimira-zelensk-55489

Zelensky, V. (2019c, November 7). Zelensky in Tesla. *YouTube.* Retrieved from https://www.youtube.com/watch?v=oyUqwB8bBGE

Zelensky, V. (2021, June 14). Interview of the president of Ukraine for foreign media. *President of Ukraine Official Website.* Retrieved from https://www.president. gov.ua/en/news/intervyu-prezidenta-ukrayini-inozemnim-zmi-69061

5 "Do Not Sell Our Motherland!"

Zelensky's Land Reform

The Motherland

Since the announcement of Ukraine's state independence in 1991, land sale has been one of the country's most hotly debated and emotionally charged issues. This is no surprise: About 70 percent of the country's surface (about 42 million hectares) has been used for agriculture, and about 75 percent of the agricultural area is arable land, two-thirds of it the agriculturally rich black soil (chernozem) (USGS, 2017). Given the country's low cost of labor, low environmental standards, and low rent for land, Ukraine's land resources have always interested potential foreign investors (Fedchyshyn et al., 2020). What has deterred many of them from investing in the agricultural sector of Ukraine was primarily the fact that the Ukrainian land market had not been liberalized.

The state monopoly on land ownership, a Soviet legacy, was abolished in Ukraine in 1992, when Ukrainian peasants gained the right to leave their collective farms and instead work individual plots of land, which they obtained from the government at no charge (Land Code, 1992). However, landowners were required to use their land only for farming, gardening, and/or house construction; they were also expected to comply with ecological and soil-protection norms, cultivate land continuously, and so forth. A failure to meet the established requirements could result in the confiscation of privately owned lands by local authorities. For advocates of a free land market, these and other restrictions were "totally inconsistent with the notion of private ownership and with market mechanisms of land management" (Csaki & Lerman, 1997, p. 2).

Various inconsistencies characterized the whole process of reforming land relations since Ukraine obtained its state independence in 1991 (Dankevych et al., 2017). Until the spring of 2020, when Volodymyr Zelensky finally managed to force the opening of the land market, it had been outlawed "to sell, donate, pledge or otherwise alienate 96% of

DOI: 10.4324/9781003228493-6

all privately owned agricultural land, as well as all state and communal lands" (Rogach et al., 2019, p. 67). Moreover, only Ukrainian citizens and Ukrainian legal entities had a right to own land (although not to sell it). As Article 22 of the Land Code (2001) of Ukraine stated, "Agricultural land cannot be transferred to the ownership of foreigners, stateless persons, foreign legal entities, and foreign states" [Іноземним громадянам та особам без громадянства земельні ділянки у власність не передаються]. When it came to land leasing, however, foreigners, stateless persons, and foreign legal entities had rights equal to those of Ukrainians (Land Lease, 1998).

Land leasing had been allowed for a term of up to 50 years. Since many small landowners could not cultivate their plots due to a lack of adequate material and financial resources (Allina-Pisano, 2004), they had to lease them to farmers or "agro-holdings"—agricultural conglomerates, "the ten largest of which have about 3 million hectares of land in their land use" (Martynyuk, 2017, p. 16). Such an enormous concentration of acreage in the hands of huge conglomerates had become possible because there were "many ways to circumvent the moratorium on agricultural land sales: long-term rent, mephitis, fictitious testament, pledge, proxy, change of land use purpose, legal foreclosure through debt, etc.," as Kurylo and colleagues (2020, p. 363) explain.

The non-transparency of the whole system of land relations allowed proponents of a free land market to argue that a market had, in fact, already been established, only in an "uncivilized" "shadow" form that prevented it from becoming a valuable resource for the country's enrichment. In the view of many land-market advocates, this had significantly impeded "the development of both the agrarian business and the inflow of investments in general, which negatively affects GDP and outflows of investments" (Fedchyshyn et al., 2020, p. 166).

The opponents of land sales see the situation in a completely different light. Despite the moratorium on land sales, they argue, the share of GDP from the agricultural sector is growing, and agricultural exports are growing as well. Given Ukraine's current trend of deindustrialization, agriculture is in fact the only growing sector of the Ukrainian economy. This is because:

> The absence of a land market allowed our farmers to save money that they would have spent on buying land… The rent is relatively low. And so they got money that they can invest in technologies, in new equipment, in new agricultural machinery—that is, in the development of their production.

[Отсутствие рынка земли позволило нашим аграриям сэкономить деньги, которые они бы тратили на выкуп земли… Арендная плата относительно невысокая. И так у них появились деньги, которые они могут вкладывать в технологии, в новое оборудование, в новую сельскохозяйственную технику—то есть, в развитие своего производства.

(Kushch, 2021, 24:23–25.04)

According to this view, the sale of land resources would enrich not Ukrainians but multinational corporations and global financial speculators (Litoshenko, 2014). Given that agricultural land comprises up to 70 percent of Ukraine's territory, the opening of the land market would deprive Ukrainians not only of soil but also of living space.

This point of view has been widely shared among Ukrainians who consider the country's soil not simply as a collective asset but as their "mother"—a metaphor found in numerous Ukrainian proverbs: "The land is our dear mother who feeds and cherishes everybody" [Земля—мати наша, всіх годує і пестить], "take care of the fertile land as you would your mother" [Доглядай землю плідну, як матір рідну], etc. It defies the wisdom of previous generations, crystallized in these maxims, to let the land go: "Do not let your land go, for your children will curse you" [Не випускай землі з рук, бо діти проклянуть] (Aphorism, n/d). These and similar Ukrainian proverbs reflect a special, almost sacred attitude of Ukrainian peasants toward their "Motherland"; it is no wonder the people's resistance against land sales has persevered. Numerous opinion polls conducted by different research centers at different times have been consistent in their findings. Most Ukrainians have been against land sales, in general, while the vast majority of them were against selling Ukrainian land to foreigners (KIIS, 2019; Rating, 2019; UHBDP, 2020).

Ukrainian presidents—Zelensky's predecessors—have advocated for the free sale of agricultural land since the implementation of a moratorium on land sales in 2001. But none of them managed to persuade the parliament of the necessity of opening the land market. Parliamentary deputies overcame presidential vetoes on several occasions or sabotaged the adoption of laws necessary to lift the moratorium and launch the market. The moratorium was prolonged several times until Zelensky and his party came to power in 2019 and established control over the Parliament (the Rada).

As outlined in Chapter 3, just three days after the new government was formed, Zelensky instructed Prime Minister Honcharuk to draft a bill to abolish the moratorium on the sale of agricultural land so that the Rada could adopt the new Land Code by December. At least two factors made this extremely rapid move a shock to many Ukrainians. First, the election program of Zelensky's party said nothing about the sale of land, while only one phrase in Zelensky's election platform described his plans for land reform: "The formation of a transparent land market" [Формування прозорого ринку землі] (Zelensky, 2019a), which could be interpreted as making existing land relations more transparent.

Moreover, in Zelensky's show *Servant of the People*, which, as I argue in Chapter 4, was used as an informal election platform, nothing at all was said about the sale of land. Quite on the contrary: Holoborodko wants to revive Ukraine's industry and space program, while the European Union insists on Ukraine's agricultural destiny. An EU representative recommends that Holoborodko abandon his "space fantasies" [давайте без космических фантазий] because "this niche is already occupied" [эта ниша уже занята] by nations with more established space programs and insists that "Eastern Europe is about agriculture" [Восточная Европа – это сельское хозяйство] (*Servant of the People*, 2019, 47:14–48:59). As a response, Holoborodko addresses the nation with a message of fiery disagreement, criticizing EU policies that keep Ukraine in its "garden" [в огороде]. "They have satellites, and we have a rake. And shovels" [У них спутники, а у нас грабли. И лопаты], he intones sarcastically, and proceeds to call on Ukrainians "to change everything" and "get real independence"—apparently from the Western institutions of power [Или может попытаться все изменить. Действительно обрести независимость] (*Servant of the People*, 2019, 53:35–54:28). These words from Holoborodko were broadcast only days before the first round of the real presidential election. For viewers of the series, encouraged to associate the ideas of Holoborodko with the candidacy of Zelensky, it could hardly have been imaginable that the real policy actions of their real president would diverge so radically from the vision provided by the show.

Although Zelensky made it clear from time to time in his very few interviews that he was not against the land market, he never elaborated on this point in any detail. This is a representative example:

> I want… all global companies to come here and invest. Actually, this is one of the alternatives to any military alliance.… We have a lot of land, many factories in a terrible state, let's give them to people, let them work! Who will take us over if there are representatives of the Arab world, China, America here?

[Я хочу… чтобы все мировые компании приезжали сюда и вкладывали. Вообще-то, это одна из альтернатив любому военному союзу…. У нас куча земли, куча заводов недобитых, которые в жутком состоянии, давайте людям дадим, пусть работают! Кто нас захватит, если тут будут представители арабского мира, Китая, Америки?].

(Zelensky, 2018, 4:58–5:39)

As is evident from this excerpt, Zelensky seems to be confident that giving away land to foreigners would be good for Ukraine as the presence of foreign investors would prevent a war against Ukraine and its occupation by an invader (although Zelensky does not say "Russia," he implies it). In other words, Zelensky links the squandering of Ukrainian soil—the main national resource—to the idea of preserving Ukraine's national sovereignty. However, as soon as the signifier "sale" is not activated, Zelensky's "give them to people, let them work" can be interpreted as a suggestion to lease land resources—not sell them.

Second, it was well-known that most Ukrainian citizens did not support opening the land market without consulting the people: "More than half of Ukrainians surveyed (64%) believe that the issue of selling agricultural land should be decided only in an all-Ukrainian referendum" [Більше половини опитаних українців (64%) вважають, що питання про продаж землі сільськогосподарського призначення має вирішуватися тільки на всеукраїнському референдумі]. (KIIS, 2019). Despite Zelensky's election promise that his first bill would establish a mechanism through which "the people of Ukraine will form the main tasks for the government through referendums and other forms of direct democracy" [Народ України буде формувати основні завдання для влади через референдуми та інші форми прямої демократії] (Zelensky, 2019a), and despite the fact that a similar promise was in the program of his party—"We will introduce mechanisms of citizens' influence on government decisions through referendums" [Запровадимо механізми впливу громадян на рішення влади через референдуми] (Program, n/d)—the "servants" decided not to wait until these mechanisms would be worked out.

As early as September 20, 2019, only three weeks after the government had been formed, the draft of the updated land legislation was published on the governmental website. The first thing experts noted was that the project provided foreigners with access to land, as the beneficiaries of Ukrainian companies, granted the right to buy land, could be foreign citizens (Kravets in Ksenz, 2019) who "will be able to exercise this right through many schemes... [such as]... buying a legal entity that has already bought land" [И реализовать это право они смогут через множество схем. Например, покупая юрлица, которые уже купили землю] (Lukash, 2019).

Ukrainian agrarians were "certainly not satisfied with the right to buy land for Ukrainian companies with the possibility of 100% capitalization from foreigners" [Нас точно не устраивает право покупать землю для украинских компаний с возможностью 100% капитализации от иностранцев], as Denis Marchuk, Deputy Head of the All-Ukrainian Agrarian Council, maintained (Muzhik, 2019). Protesting the law proposed by Zelensky's government, agrarians demanded: "Do not sell the Motherland!" [Не продавайте Родину!] (Mogilevich, 2019). With this and similar slogans like "No land sale for foreigners!" [Нет продаже земли иностранцам!] they blocked highways, picketed the Rada, and skirmished with police.

Agrarians were especially outraged by the fact that the government had been rushing headlong toward opening the land market without adopting the necessary laws for it to operate transparently: that is, laws regarding the land cadastre, preferential loans for farmers, the prevention of raiding, and so forth. Before opening the market, the protesters argued, the government should put everything in order so that farmers would be guaranteed cheap credit and protected from the threats of landlessness, raiders, and monopolization. The huge maximum amount of land privatization allowed by the proposed law—up to 200,000 hectares per owner—was especially resented by small farmers, as it would legalize the consolidation of land ownership by agrarian oligarchs, both Ukrainian and foreign. "Two hundred people will be able to buy the whole of Ukraine!" [Это 200 человек могут скупить всю Украину!]—this was an emotional response to the proposed norm by one of the farmers (Gubrienko, 2019).

Under pressure from the protests, Zelensky had to make a tactical retreat. "The situation with this law is difficult," he acknowledged on October 10, 2019, during a press conference:

> I met with many farmers, I heard them, red lines were identified... Now I am saying that in no case should this law be brought to the Rada. For some time, we must sell land only to Ukrainians. Then you can open it to foreign companies.

> [Ситуация с земельным законом сложная. Я нашел время и встретился со многими фермерами, я их услышал, «красные линии» увидели. Сейчас я говорю, что ни в коем случае нельзя нести этот закон в Верховную Раду. Некоторое время

мы должны продавать землю только украинцам…Потом уже можно открыть рынок земли другим иностранным компаниям].
(Reporter.ua, 2019)

Zelensky also agreed that the decision as to whether foreigners could buy Ukrainian land should be made by the Ukrainian people in a referendum—the main demand of most Ukrainians and opposition parties.

The final version of the Land Code,[1] which was adopted on March 31, 2020, contained important changes as compared to its initial version released half a year earlier. The opening of the land market was scheduled for July 1, 2021; however, only Ukrainian citizens could buy land and the limit was set at 100 hectares per owner during the first two years. Starting from January 1, 2024, Ukrainian legal entities will be allowed to purchase land, but can only consolidate a maximum of 10,000 hectares. It was decided that foreigners would have to wait until a national referendum grants them the right to purchase land within Ukrainian territory (Government Portal, 2020).

Against the People's Will

Despite these changes, most Ukrainians did not approve the adoption of the law (KIIS, 2020). In line with public sentiment, opposition parties have been arguing that the law is unconstitutional,[2] that the process of adopting the law was riddled with procedural violations, that the decision was made without consulting the people of Ukraine, and that it defies the will of most Ukrainian citizens. Although the law states that until 2024 land is allowed to be sold only to individuals, critics argue that peasants and small farmers do not have the resources to buy land, and the mechanisms to protect their interests (laws to deter raiders and ensure low-cost bank loans, etc.) have yet to be developed. Critical voices maintain that under these circumstances, only large holdings, oligarchs, corrupted officials, and criminals will be able to buy land—those who have money and the ability to protect their investments in a lawless environment without state protection. They can do so through transferring purchase rights to proxies and forcing poor villagers to sell their plots for almost nothing.

Additionally, the new law has transformed banks into the largest latifundia owners—a change that, according to Alexei Kushch, a Kyiv-based economist, was intended from the very beginning:

Banks, including those with foreign capital, have received a unique opportunity to concentrate land, moreover, without any restrictions on its size. But banks are an outpost of speculative capital.... Banks can offer various financial instruments—land certificates, mutual funds, etc.

[Банки, в том числе, с иностранным капиталом, получили уникальную возможность концентрировать землю, причем, безо всяких ограничений по объемам. Но банки и есть форпостом спекулятивного капитала.... Банки могут предлагать различные финансовые инструменты под землю – скажем, земельные сертификаты, создавать фонды паевого участия и прочее].

(Kushch in Ksenz, 2020)

Because not everyone will be able to make loan payments, and many farmers, without state protection, will simply go broke, the law threatens to leave villagers landless as their plots go to land speculators, including foreign ones, Kushch maintains.

Given all the pitfalls and potential dangers for common Ukrainians that came with the law, most farmers did not welcome its adoption. Moreover, as they argued, it was impossible to open the land market at a time of deep economic crisis, when the value of any asset decreases sharply. On the eve of the law's adoption, the All-Ukrainian Agrarian Rada demanded that the launch of the land market be postponed until the economic situation had stabilized. The concerns of the Agrarian Rada went unheeded, as did the concerns of the parliamentary opposition, whom Arakhamia, leader of the parliamentary faction of the "servants," called "buzzing insects" (more on this in Chapter 6). The oppositional "buzzing" has been effectively silenced by the roar of the "servant" party engine. Here is a very telling excerpt from a talk show in which the land reform was discussed:

YULIA TYMOSHENKO (leader of the "Batkivshchyna" party): The model that is now being imposed on us by this law is the model that has been used in several countries, such as Madagascar and Argentina, and it has had very serious consequences for those countries.... Ukrainian land will become essentially a bargaining chip for global players and for monopolies within the country....

[Та модель, яка нам зараз навязується цим законом – це та модель, яка була використана в декількох країнах таких як Мадагаскар, Аргентина—вона привела для дуже тяжких наслідків для цих країн.... Українська земля стане по суті розмінною монетою для глобальних гравців і для монополій всередені країни].

DENYS SHMYHAL (Prime Minister of Ukraine): The land market exists all over the world. The issue of the land market model is a debatable issue, indeed; it needs to be discussed and is being discussed now in parliament....

[Ринок землі існує в усьому світі. Питання моделі ринку землі – це дійсно дискусійне питання, яке повинно обговорюватися і обговорюється зараз в парламенті]

TYMOSHENKO: I would like to inform you that there is no debate in the parliament. There is a bill prepared outside the parliament, prepared by completely speculative financial groups of a global scale. It was imposed on the parliament. No amendment made in light of world experience is adopted by parliament.... This law stipulates that foreign banks will own Ukrainian agricultural land.... In fact, we sell Ukrainian land once and for all. We are leaving ourselves without profit, without quality food, without farming, without anything.

[Я вас інформую, що в парламенті дискусії немає. Є підготовлений за межами парламента законопроект. Підготовлений абсолютно спекулятивними фінансовими групами глобального масштабу. Навязали це парламенту. Жодна правка, яка напрацьована з оглядом на світовий досвід, не приймається парламентом. В цьому законі закладено, що іноземні банки будуть володіти українською сільськогосподарською землею... Фактично ми один раз і на все життя продаємо українську землю. Ми залишаємо нас без прибутку, без якісних продуктів харчування, без фермерства, без нічого].

SHMYHAL: Dear Ukrainians. We are not going to sell Ukrainian land. We give the right to Ukrainians to dispose of their land.... We want to give Ukrainians the right to sell land. This is not a duty. This is just an opportunity. It is a legal opportunity to dispose of it. Everything else is a matter of popular referendum.

[Шановні Українці. Ми не збираємося продавати українську землю. Ми даємо право українцям розпоряджатися своїм.... Ми хочемо дати українцям право продавати землю. Це не обовязок. Це лише можливість. Законна можливість цим розпоряджатися. Все решта—це вже питання народного референдуму].

(Shmyhal, 2020, 23:27–30:23)

As is evident from this excerpt, the opposition, as represented on this TV show by Tymoshenko, articulated the land reform through its linkages to global financial speculation, the potential impoverishment of

Ukrainians, the loss of Ukraine's sovereignty, and the collective right of the people of Ukraine to negotiate the details of the legislation. Prime Minister Shmyhal also framed the issue in terms of people's rights; but in his interpretation, these "rights" were conceptualized extremely narrowly—exclusively in terms of the individual right to sell (more on this in Chapter 6). Ostensibly, he was not against parliamentary discussions; however, with the party apparatus of the "servants" controlling parliament, there was no possibility for further discussion or negotiation.

Given that the party machine used by the "servants" to push their neoliberal reforms has been formed on the fringes of the virtual and the real, it is pertinent to recall that the series *Servant of the People* portrayed Tymoshenko (through the character Zhanna Borisenko) as an extremely corrupted politician who cares only about her personal well-being and haute couture clothing (see Chapter 3).[3] As the next chapter shows, the Ukrainian people's opposition to land sales has been interpreted by Zelensky exclusively as manipulations carried out by such corrupted "old politicians" who "intimidate ordinary people" by "planting myths in their heads" [Старі політики залякали простих людей. Посіяли у їх головах ряд міфів] (Zelensky, 2019b, 1:40–1:50).

On April 21, 2021, under pressure from international institutions advocating for the land market (Mousseau & Teare, 2019), the Cabinet of Ministers approved a bill on amendments to the law on the consolidation of agricultural land, providing grounds for the compulsory consolidation of land shares. Now, if the owner of a small share does not want to voluntarily sell or exchange it, the transaction can be forced in court (Law Project, 2021). According to the new bill, the owners of small land shares whose plots "hinder the optimization of land use" can be offered redemption, the "equivalent exchange" of plots, as well as changes to existing lease agreements; the bill does not explain, however, what an "equivalent exchange" would be. This and other governmental decisions related to land sales have provided grounds for critics to claim that the process of preparing land plots for sale to large buyers had already begun, and that small owners would be forced out earlier than planned initially.

According to Kushch (2021), the goal of current political elites is to create uncomfortable conditions for small landowners, such as unaffordable prices for land and exorbitant taxes for using it. Under this pressure, peasants will be forced to sell their lands at low prices, allowing profiteers to consolidate land plots into large tracts and eventually reap great profits by selling them to Western companies once the market is open to foreigners. As Kushch explains,

> Very large financial lobbies in the West are behind the land market opening. Western pension funds [and] investment funds want to invest money... Money depreciates... Investors are now actively looking for some assets to invest in...A very large amount is at stake to open this land market.

> [За открытием рынка земли стоят очень крупные финансовые лобби Запада. Пенсионные фонды инвестиционные фонды запада, которые хотят вложить деньги... Деньги обесцениваются... Поэтому инвесторы сейчас активно ищут какие-то активы, в которые можно вложить деньги...Очень большие деньги поставлены на кон.].
>
> (Kushch, 2021, 6:40–7:26]

"Get ready for consolidation—they will not ask you" [Готовьтесь к консолидации—вас никто не будет спрашивать], Kushch concludes.

Indeed, the opinions of Ukrainians, which amount to massive public opposition to land sales—at least, in the version proposed by the "servants"—have hardly been taken into account. It seems to have been much more important for Zelensky and those around him to get approval from his Western "partners"—the IMF, the World Bank, EBRD, etc.—that "have been aggressively laying the groundwork for the large-scale privatization of land and the expansion of industrial agriculture in Ukraine" (Mousseau & Teare, 2019). All of these "partners" have welcomed the sale of Ukrainian soil, arguing that it "will create enormous opportunities for prosperity" [створить величезні можливості для процвітання] (G7AmbReformUA, 2019)—as a tweet from G-7 ambassadors put it, suggesting prosperity for all Ukrainians despite the various structural inequalities highlighted by the opposition. Given that in any market there will always be losers as well as winners, the implausible promises made by G-7 and other advocates of Ukraine's neoliberalization appeared to be nothing more than euphemized constructions, delinking the signifier "land sale" from any negative consequences of the reform and connecting it instead to "prosperity for all"—a well-known neoliberal mythology (Dean, 2009).

As the next chapter will show, the "servants" also employed this kind of euphemized discourse—a promise of universal prosperity—to sell their land reform plans to Ukrainians. However, it was much more common for them to hide their neoliberal agenda by employing the discourse of historical progress—using, in this case, its specific anti-Communist version. The next chapter will discuss this in more detail.

Notes

1 In the spring of 2021, a new bill on amendments to the Land Code was adopted.
2 Article 13 of the Constitution of Ukraine states that the land, its sub-soil, atmosphere, water and other natural resources within the territory of Ukraine, the natural resources of its continental shelf, and the exclusive (maritime) economic zone, are objects of the right of property of the Ukrainian people"; Article 14 provides that "land is the fundamental national wealth that is under special state protection" (Constitution, 1996).
3 To be sure, Tymoshenko's reputation can hardly be called squeaky clean. The history of her business and political success can be traced back to the infamous 1990s, when she founded a company controlling gas supplies from Russia, which made her one of the richest people in Ukraine (Meek, 2004). At various times, the "gas princess" has been accused of violations of the Criminal Code and was twice imprisoned—under the rule of President Kuchma in 2001 and President Yanukovych in 2011—but all the charges were later dropped as politically motivated. Tymoshenko's questionable reputation does not mean, however, that her arguments against the land reform are untenable and should be dismissed.

References

Allina-Pisano, J. (2004). Land reform and the social origins of private farmers in Russia and Ukraine. *The Journal of Peasant Studies, 31*(3/4), 489–514. doi: 10.1080/0306615042000262661

Aphorism. (n/d). Прислів'я, приказки / Українські [Proverbs, sayings / Ukrainian]. Retrieved from http://www.aphorism.org.ua/subrazd.php?page=246&pages_block=17&rid=2&sid=16

Constitution. (1996). Constitution of Ukraine. Retrieved from https://www.refworld.org/pdfid/44a280124.pdf

Csaki, C., & Lerman, Z. (1997). Land reform in Ukraine: The first five years. *The World Bank*. Retrieved from https://documents1.worldbank.org/curated/en/936661468319489762/pdf/multi-page.pdf

Dankevych, E., Dankevych, V., & Chaikin, O. (2017). Ukraine agricultural land market formation preconditions. *Acta Universitatis Agriculturae et Silviculturae Mendelianae Brunensis, 65*(1), 259–271.

Dean, J. (2009). *Democracy and other neoliberal fantasies*. Durham, NC & London: Duke University Press.

Fedchyshyn, D., Ignatenko, I., & Leiba, L. (2020). Land-use rights for agricultural land in Ukraine. *Ius Humani. Law Journal, 9*(1), 159–178. doi: 10.31207/ih.v9i1.215

G7AmbReformUA. (2019, May 20). Послы G7 вітають прийняття... [The G7 ambassadors welcome the adoption...] *Twitter*. Retrieved from https://twitter.com/g7ambreformua/status/1395349738770386952

Government Portal. (2020, March 31). Verkhovna Rada of Ukraine voted for the opening of land market. Retrieved from https://www.kmu.gov.ua/en/news/verhovna-rada-ukrayini-progolosuvala-za-vidkrittya-rinku-zemli

Gubrienko, R. (2019, November 3). Алкоголики продадут паи за бутылку водки [Alcoholics will sell shares for a bottle of vodka]. *Strana.ua*. Retrieved from https://strana.ua/articles/analysis/230217-dialoh-pro-ukrainu-po-rehionam-s-ahitatsiej-za-rynok-zemli-poekhali-zamministra-ekonomicheskoho-razvitija-taras-vysotskij-polpred-zelenskoho-roman-leshchenko-i-ekspert-serhej-bilenko.html

KIIS. (2019, September 26). Оцінка населенням України деяких політичних подій вересня 2019 року [Assessment by the population of Ukraine of some political events in September 2019]. *Kyiv International Institute of Sociology*. Retrieved from https://www.kiis.com.ua/?lang=eng&cat=reports&id=894&page=9

KIIS. (2020, February 27). Оцінка діяльності органів влади та реакція на актуальні події [Evaluation of government activities and reaction to current events]. *Kyiv International Institute of Sociology*. Retrieved from https://www.kiis.com.ua/?lang=eng&cat=reports&id=920&page=6

Ksenz, L. (2019, September 21). Большой земельный передел [Large land redistribution]. *Strana.ua*. Retrieved from https://strana.ua/articles/analysis/223509-bolshoj-zemelnyj-peredel-kak-u-ze-budut-rasprodavat-ukrainskie-chernozemy-i-komu-v-itohe-oni-dostanutsja.html

Ksenz, L. (2020, January 14). 10 тисяч в одни руки и банковский "безлимит" [10 thousand in one hand and bank "unlimited"]. *KN-Partners*. Retrieved from https://knpartners.com.ua/10-tyisyach-v-odni-ruki-i-bankovskiy-bezlimit-kak-perepisali-proekt-po-prodazhe-zemli-i-kakie-lazeyki-tam-poyavilis/

Kurylo, M., Lukash, S., Ladyka, Y., Zakharova, O., & Sopyanenko, O. (2020). Contents and risks of land reform in Ukraine. *Problems and Perspectives in Management, 18*(1), 359–370. doi: 10.21511/ppm.18(1).2020.31

Kushch, A. (2021, June 10). Рынок земли—одна из самых больших ошибок нынешней власти [The land market is one of the biggest mistakes of the current government]. YouTube. Retrieved from https://www.youtube.com/watch?v=YTOs7ThtLFo

Land Code. (1992). Про внесення змін і доповнень до Земельного кодексу Української РСР [On modifications and additions to Land Code of the Ukrainian SSR]. Retrieved from https://zakon.rada.gov.ua/laws/show/2196-12#Text

Land Code. (2001). Земельний кодекс України [Law land of Ukraine]. *Verkhovna Rada*. Retrieved from http://extwprlegs1.fao.org/docs/pdf/ukr43459.pdf

Land Lease. (1998). Про оренду землі [On Land Lease]. *Verkhovna Rada.* Retrieved from https://zakon.rada.gov.ua/laws/show/161-14/print

Law Project. (2021, April 28). Проект Закону про внесення змін до деяких законодавчих актів України з питань консолідації земель [Draft law on amendments to certain legislative acts of Ukraine on land consolidation]. *Verkhovna Rada.* Retrieved from https://w1.c1.rada.gov.ua/pls/zweb2/webproc4_1?pf3511=71783

Litoshenko, O. (2014). The problem of the moratorium on the sale of agricultural land. *Legal Regulation of the Economy, 14,* 284–293.

Lukash, O. (2019, September 21). Проанализировала проект Закона Украины [Analyzing the draft law of Ukraine]. *Facebook.* Retrieved from https://www.facebook.com/ElenaLukash.ua/posts/2184330521866312/

Martynyuk, M. (2017). Agricultural land market in Ukraine: State and prospects of introduction. *Ekonomika APK, 3,* 15–21.

Meek, J. (2004, November 26). The millionaire revolutionary. *Guardian.* Retrieved from https://www.theguardian.com/world/2004/nov/26/ukraine.gender

Mogilevich, D. (2019, October 3). "Не продавайте Родину": Под ВР аграрии протестуют против продажи земли иностранцам ["Do not sell your Motherland": Under BP, agrarians protest against the sale of land to foreigners]. *Dengi.ua.* Retrieved from https://dengi.ua/finance/1821026-ne-prodavajte-rodinu-pod-vr-agrarii-protestujut-protiv-prodazhi-zemli-inostrancam

Mousseau, F., & Teare, E. (2019, November 13). Ukraine, the land of quid pro quos. *Common Dreams.* Retrieved from https://www.commondreams.org/views/2019/11/13/ukraine-land-quid-pro-quos

Muzhik, A. (2019, September 19). Большой земельный передел [Large land redistribution]. *Zhitomir.Life.* Retrieved from https://zhitomir.life/blogy/bol-shoj-zemel-nyj-peredel-kak-u-ze-budut-rasprodavat-ukrainskie-chernozemy-i-komu-v-itoge-oni-dostanutsya.html

Program. (n/d). Передвиборна програма партії "Слуга Народу" [The election platform of "Servant of the People" party]. *Servant of the People.* Retrieved from https://sluganarodu.com/program

Rating. (2019, October 30). Отдельные аспекты отношения населения к земельному вопросу [Certain aspects of the attitude of the population to the land issue]. Retrieved from http://ratinggroup.ua/ru/research/ukraine/otdelnye_aspekty_otnosheniya_naseleniya_k_zemelnomu_voprosu.html

Reporter.ua. (2019, October 11). Пресс-марафон Зеленского [Zelensky's press-marathon].Retrieved from https://reporter-ua.com/2019/10/11/351938_press-marafon-zelenskogo-korotko-o-glavnom

Rogach, S., Sulima, N., Gutsul, T., & Ilkiv, L. (2019). *Agricultural economics: Textbook.* Kyiv: Comprint.

Servant of the People. (2019, March 29). Season 3, Episode 3. *YouTube.* Retrieved from https://www.youtube.com/watch?v=iAFQGw8RM-g

Shmyhal, D. (2020, March 5). Political talk-show "The Right to Power." *YouTube.* Retrieved from https://www.youtube.com/watch?v=ovI-PvUNGoA

UHBDP. (2020, April 22). Ukraine to open land market: attitude of stakeholders in UHBDP Survey. *Ukraine Horticulture Business Development Project.* Retrieved from https://uhbdp.org/en/2198-ukraine-to-open-land-market-attitude-of-stakeholders-in-uhbdp-survey

USGS. (2017). New map of worldwide croplands supports food and water security. *U.S. Geological Survey.* Retrieved from https://www.usgs.gov/news/new-map-worldwide-croplands-supports-food-and-water-security

Zelensky, V. (2018, December 25). В гостях у Дмитрия Гордона [Visiting Dmytro Gordon]. *YouTube.* Retrieved from https://www.youtube.com/watch?v=VPE2hv8qbBc

Zelensky, V. (2019a, n/d). Передвиборча програма кандидата на пост Президента України Володимира Зеленського [Election program of the candidate for President of Ukraine Volodymyr Zelensky]. Retrieved from https://program.ze2019.com/

Zelensky, V. (2019b, November 11). Срочное обращение президента Зеленского [An urgent address of President Zelensky]. *YouTube.* Retrieved from https://www.youtube.com/watch?v=tE_V6PxPYA8

6 "To Bury Communism"

A Failure of the Modernization Rhetoric of the "Servants"

The Communist Specter

The Communist Party of Ukraine—one of the most influential parties of post-Soviet times and the most strident opponent of land commodification—was prohibited from participating in the parliamentary elections after the victory of the Euromaidan. The prohibition stemmed from the decommunization legislation adopted in 2015. By the time Zelensky's land reform came to be approved by the parliament, the Communist Party—along with its voters who were deprived of a channel for voicing their concerns—had lost the opportunity to influence the parliamentary process. However, the Communist specter still seems to haunt the "servants," who have been promoting their land reform predominantly as an anti-Communist/anti-Soviet civilizational crusade.

In their "civilizational" story line, those opposing the land sales appeared not as political opponents highlighting the negative aspects of a very specific proposed reform, but as people with a backward, Soviet ("sovok") mentality who ostensibly opposed reforms of any kind. This is how Zelensky commented on attempts to extend the moratorium on land sales during a conference on the land reform in September 2019:

> Sorry, but here is the Soviet Union again. This is where *sovok* starts. This is where we, the citizens, allegedly got our apartments, but could not sell them legally.

> [Інакше це—вибачте—з'являється у нас Радянський Союз. Починається совок. Коли ми, громаняни, отримали ніби-то отримали свої квартири але не могли продавати їх легально].
> (Zelensky, 2019a, 9:21–9:34)

DOI: 10.4324/9781003228493-7

As is evident from Zelensky's discursive construction, his negative emotions about the "sovok" condition are primarily about the fact that Soviet citizens were unable to sell their apartments, which they had received from the state free of charge. Apparently, he did not see the difference between selling apartments, which can be built from scratch or reconstructed at any time, and land, which can never be renewed or replaced—a factor presupposing a very careful consideration of all the possible consequences of its sale. No careful consideration was evident in Zelensky's speech, which presented the issue as a simple dichotomy between "the good" (understood as "the modern") and "the bad" (the "outdated"/the Soviet).

Having nothing to do with reality (to put it simply, there was no way to return to the USSR by rejecting the land reform as proposed by the "servants"), this mythological construction, however, was supported by Zelensky's team unconditionally. "I support the land reform. It's high time to get rid of the *sovok*" [Я підтримую земельну реформу. Треба вже закінчувати цей совок], said the Minister of the Cabinet of Ministers Dmytro Dubilet (2019), echoing Zelensky. Like the president, Dubilet equated the lack of a land market with Soviet rule, as if the USSR had not ceased to exist three decades before the "servants" came to power, and as if present-day Ukraine, after years of rampant privatization and the dissolution of the Soviet welfare system, could still be characterized as "Soviet."

Poturaev (2019) was more eloquent. "Ukraine will finally bury communism," he shouted from the parliamentary podium:

> We will finally settle accounts with this maniac Lenin, with the cannibal Stalin, who did everything to deprive the Ukrainian people of the main wealth—land. We will return the land to Ukrainians once and for all!
>
> [Україна остаточно поховає комунізм! Ми нарешті зведемо рахунки з цим маньяком Леніним! Із людожером Сталіним! Які зробили все, щоб позбавити українців головного багатства—землі!]
>
> (Puturaev, 2019, 0:08–1:57)

As is clear from this construction, for Poturaev, "to deprive Ukrainians of the land" was equal to "not allowing Ukrainians to sell it," while "to return the land to Ukrainians" meant "to allow Ukrainians the right to sell it." The manipulative character of this construction is obvious. Indeed, under Soviet rule, peasants were deprived of the opportunity to sell and buy land; they were denied many other freedoms as well. In fact, until 1974, Soviet peasants did not have passports and required special permission just to leave their villages. Under such circumstances, the right to sell land would have been useless without first obtaining more basic rights. However—a paradoxical development—it was the Soviet system of collective farming that ultimately provided Ukrainians with an opportunity to preserve their lands for future generations. Precisely because it was forbidden to sell national land resources under the Soviet rule, Ukrainian peasants received their land plots—free of charge—after the Soviet Union ceased to exist. In the 1990s, their land did not go to banks and financial speculators. It was only three decades later that such a development became possible—after Zelensky's party machine captured full control of parliament and forced through the new land code, amid a high level of disapproval among the public.

In the imagination of the "servants," it was exactly the "outdated" and "immoral" Communist-Soviet tradition—not to sell "the fundamental national wealth" and "property of the Ukrainian people" (Constitution, 1996)—that had prevented Ukraine from "moving forward" and catching up with more advanced societies characterized by full-fledged markets. "The world is moving forward, and... we are lagging behind" [Мир уходит вперед.... мы отстаем]—this is how Tymofiy Mylovanov (2019a), the Minister of Economic Development, Trade and Agriculture, commented on the lack of a land market in Ukraine. As in the previous examples, the essence of the issue—the land sale reform broadly opposed by the public—was euphemized in the discourse of historical forward movement along the avenue of progress, in the company of civilized elders. As outlined in Chapter 1, the narrative of civilization and historical progress has been the main euphemizing device masking the reality of neoliberal transformations in post-Soviet Ukraine since its independence, and the "servants" simply used a well-worn track.

Employing the discourse of unidirectional historical progress—a movement away from the "*sovok*," with its collective ownership of national resources, to the "normal" civilizational future of buying and selling—allowed post-Soviet reformers to present themselves as aligned with the "progressive avant-garde of history," signified by an imaginary unitary West, as opposed to the "forces of the past" represented by economically less-developed countries which forbid land commodification. During his speech at a conference on the land reform in September 2019, Zelensky (2019a) argued:

> The list of countries—you know this quite well—where there is no land market is well known. These are North Korea, Tajikistan, Venezuela, Cuba, Congo, Ukraine—congratulations!

[Список країн—ви це прекрасно знаєте – де немає ринку землі, всім відомий. Це Північна Корея, Таджикістан, Венесуела, Куба, Конго, Україна—вітаю]

(10:57–11:13)

Zelensky's "Congratulations!" was a sarcastic jab at Ukraine's presence among the world's least economically advanced countries, whose "uncivilized" condition was illustrated by the absence of a land market. United equivalentially, these countries comprised a totality of historical barbarism—the radical outside of the community of progressive civilized states, in which, as Zelensky acknowledged, "different models of the market exist":

Foreigners [in "normal" civilized states] can or cannot buy the land—but the market nevertheless exists. Farmers may take loans secured by their land, enlarge their farms, attract investments…

[Іноземці можуть, або не можуть купувати землю. Але сам ринок існує. Фермери можуть брати кредити від землю. Розширювати своє господарство. Залучати інвестиції].

(Zelensky, 2019b, 1:13–1:32)

Again, what is seen in this construction is Zelensky's valorization of the market, which he presents as a signature of civilization, while at the same time he completely ignores all of its problematic aspects. The question of how (i.e., at whose expense) farms can be "enlarged" is left without consideration. In line with the neoliberal fantasy of "prosperity for all," Zelensky and those around him promised that all Ukrainians would enrich themselves through selling land, while simultaneously valorizing the idea of growth ("to enlarge farms"). Given that the amount of land is limited, and that the enlargement of somebody's holdings will inevitably mean the diminution of another's, the promise of general enrichment made by Zelensky appears to be another euphemizing construct hiding the essence of his neoliberal reformation, which has little to do with the general well-being of all Ukrainians.

The idea of growth, presented as an antithesis to Soviet statism, has been central to all the discursive constructions of Zelensky's close allies. As Honcharuk (2019a) put it while speaking to agrarians during a conference on the land reform,

For our country to be successful, we need to grow 5–7 percent a year. To grow 5–7 percent a year, we desperately need to lift all the

Soviet restrictions that we now have. The restriction that exists on the real, legal sale of land is one of them.

[Для того, щоб наша країна була успішною, нам треба зростати 5–7 відсотків на рік. Для того, щоб зростати 5–7 відсотків на рік, нам вкрай необхідно познімати всі ті радянські обмеження, які у нас зараз існують. Обмеження, яке існує на реальний, легальний продаж землі—це один з них].

(Honcharuk, 2019a, 11:05–11:30)

As with the examples discussed earlier, the logic of Honcharuk's construction does not hold up under critical scrutiny. There were several years in the history of post-Soviet Ukraine when annual GDP growth was more than 5 percent, the minimum goal set by Honcharuk; these years were from 2000 to 2004, 2006 and 2007, and 2011. In 2006 and 2007, GDP growth was more than 7 percent; in 2001 and 2003, more than 9 percent; and in 2004, almost 12 percent (World Bank, n/d). Apparently, land sales were not necessary for this GDP growth to take place, contrary to Honcharuk's claim. What was necessary was the development of the industrial potentiality of Ukraine, which the country inherited from the Soviet Union—an economic sector in which most of the "servants," including Honcharuk, have no expertise.[1] The decline of industrial output under the rule of the "servants" is telling: In April 2020, when the government of Honcharuk was dismissed, it had reached the point of −16 percent (BNE Intellinews, 2020). "Servant" discourse about moving away from the "sovok" condition not only euphemized the neoliberal essence of their reforms, but also masked the fact that—regardless of their prowess at financial speculation (see Chapter 8)—they were incompetent at managing a real economy.[2]

The Battle for Stalingrad

As for the leaders of opposition parties protesting the reform, in the representation of Zelensky and his allies they have appeared exclusively as crooks who have been profiting from "a large-scale thriving shadow market" [масштабний процвітаючий тіньовий ринок], as Mylovanov (2019a) put it. In Honcharuk's view,

We are not old politicians who have been extending the moratorium for eight consecutive convocations from year to year, encouraging the sale of land through "gray" schemes for a pittance and renting it for a penny.

[Мы—не старые политики, которые уже восемь созывов подряд из года в год продлевали мораторий, поощряя за бесценок продавать через "серые" схемы землю и сдавать ее в аренду за копейки].

(Honcharuk, 2019b)

The fact that opposition politicians who protest the reform are called "old" is suggestive: Whether they are involved in "gray schemes" or not, the implication is that their time is over. All their attempts to preserve the past and prevent the "normal" future from coming were destined to fail, simply because "the old" always gives way to "the new"—such is the law of nature. According to this "natural law," the younger generation of reformers is destined to serve as a historical avant-garde, with its grand mission being to help Ukraine catch up with a civilizational "norm" equated to the Western/neoliberal condition.

Presented as morally degraded, corrupted, and outdated, the "old politicians" opposing the land reform were described by Poturaev (2019) as:

The descendants of Yagoda, Yezhov and Beria[3]—the bloody executioners of the Ukrainian people—the descendants of those who staged the Holodomor, who killed millions of Ukrainians by depriving them of their land!

[Нащадки Ягоди, Єжова, Берії – кровавих катів українського народу! Оці люди – вони нащадки тих, хто влаштовував Голодомор! Хто вбив мільйони українців, позбавив їх цемлі].

"Here they are! Here they are!"—screamed Poturaev from the parliamentary tribune, pointing at the opposition factions in the parliamentary hall:

Minions of Russia, which staged the Holodomor here and killed Ukrainians… Here they are again trying to deprive Ukrainians of land! They want a Muscovite boot to come here again! And to starve everyone, but no! Today, we will end this once and for all! Today, we will return the land to the people! Today we will return the land to every Ukrainian! Land to the people! Land to Ukrainians!

[Ось вони! Ось вони! Міньйони Росії, яка влаштувала тут Голодомор і вбила українців… Ось вони знову намагаються позбавити українців землі! Вони знову хочуть, щоб сюди прийшов московитний сапог! І морив усіх голодом, але ні! Сьогодні ми з цим покінчемо раз і назавжди! Сьогодні ми повернемо народу землю! Сьогодні ми повернемо кожному українцю землю! Землю людям! Землю українцям!]

(Poturaev, 2019, 0:08–1:57)

Not only did Poturaev equate the right to sell the land with the possession of land (as in his previous message, analyzed earlier), but he also united equivalentially the lack of a right to sell the land and the atrocity of Holodomor—the great hunger that Stalin created by expropriating peasants' crops to cover needs during Soviet industrialization. From Poturaev's construction, it seemed as if Holodomor happened not because Stalin expropriated crops, but because peasants did not have a right to sell their land. Given that peasants did not have the right to leave their collective farms, it is not clear how land sales could have saved them from Stalinism, but it is obvious that Poturaev's performance was meant to shift the focus of the discussion away from the essence of the issue (the pros and cons of the specific land reform pushed forward by "servants") to the immorality of the Soviet regime and its "descendants." The opposition was presented not as people with alternative political views, but as the heirs to Stalin's politics of repressing peasants.

In other words, instead of defining the confrontation in political categories, the "servants" presented it in moral terms, an intentional tactic—clearly, none of those opposing Zelensky's land reform had anything to do with Stalinism. The mythological constructions of Poturaev and other "servants" presenting the opposition as "the descendants of Yagoda, Yezhov, and Beria" are perfectly in line with what Mouffe (2005) dubbed "the moralistic tendency of the post-political Zeitgeist" (p. 4). By articulating the opposition as a homogeneous mass that was essentially amoral, non-modern, and radically different from Zelensky's reformers with their "progressive" neoliberal agenda, the latter created the conditions for "maximum separation," to put it in Laclau and Mouffe's terms, where "no element in the system of equivalences enters into relations other than those of opposition to the elements of the other system" (1985, p. 129). When this condition is reached, "two societies" appear in place of one, and the confrontation between these "societies" becomes "fierce, total and indiscriminate: there exist no discourses capable of establishing differences within an equivalential chain in which each and every one of its elements symbolizes evil" (Laclau & Mouffe, 1985, p. 129).

Indeed, the confrontation with the opposition with respect to the land reform had come to be presented as a fight between good and evil, a stance which did not presuppose any political solution—only war to the bitter end, as in the battle of Stalingrad between the Red Army and the Wehrmacht:

> The battle for Stalingrad begins... Every voice is important. Now let's extend the working day and fight.
>
> [Битва за Сталинград начинается. Прошу всех в зал. Каждый голос, каждый важен. Сейчас продлим рабочий день и будем сражаться].
>
> (Kvitka, 2019)

This is how Arakhamia motivated his colleagues to vote for the new Land Code in its first reading. He also compared the opposition to an "insect"—a metaphor that does not presuppose the possibility of negotiation. According to Arakhamia, the opposition was like a "little insect that flies and buzzes a lot... but does not have any influence on the process" [маленька якась комаха, яка літає і дзижчить багато... але ніякого впливу на цей процес не має] (Arakhamia, 2020, 0:05–0:15). The oppositional "insect," albeit annoying, has indeed appeared harmless—the party machine of the "servants" has been effective at defending them against oppositional bites.

The only thing to disappoint Zelensky amid the success of his parliamentary machine has been the people's unwavering perseverance in rejecting the party's neoliberal initiatives. Taught by the bitter experience of the post-Soviet reforms, most Ukrainians stubbornly refused to believe that new neoliberal experiments would bring prosperity to all. The well-established narrative about "bad old politicians" manipulating people turned out to be very useful here. "This issue has been manipulated for the last 20 years," Zelensky (2019b) claimed:

> Old politicians intimidated ordinary people. They planted several myths in their heads. Convincing people that this cannot be done. Aren't you surprised that old politicians started taking care of the people? And maybe the question is different? Maybe they are lobbying someone's interests? The interests of those who simply benefit from Ukrainians not owning land. Just think of it.
>
> [Старі політики залякали простих людей. Посіяли у їх головах ряд міфів. Переконуючи, що цього не можна робити. А вас не дивує, що старі політики почали піклуватися про народ? А

можливо питання в іншому? Можливо, вони лобіюють чиїсь
інтереси? Інтереси тих, кому просто вигідно, щоб українці не
володіли землею. Просто подумайте].

(Zelensky, 2019b, 1:40–2:14)

"Horror stories about Chinese, Arabs, or aliens taking our land out by
wagons is a delusion," argued Zelensky [Страшилки про китайців,
арабів або інопланетян, які вивезуть нашу землю вагонами—це
маячня] (2019a, 8:38–8:47), apparently forgetting his own pre-election
interviews, in which he—not "old politicians"—suggested to give away
Ukraine's land to foreigners, hoping their investments would serve to
defend Ukraine against Russia (see Chapter 5). In line with a classic
excuse for all political failures—"dammit, we ought to have won …
but we didn't, so they must've manipulated the masses" (Hartley, 1992,
p. 26)—Zelensky explained the people's disapproval of the land reform
exclusively in terms of the scary tales disseminated by "old politicians."

This is how Zelensky commented on the clashes over the land reform
that took place near the building of the Rada on December 17, 2019,
when 17 law enforcement officers were injured:

> I respect the opinion of Ukrainians, for months we have been lis-
> tening to proposals for reforms. However, at the rally on the land
> law, it was not the voices of farmers, but political slogans that were
> heard. We listen to people. And this is how Ukraine will move
> towards a better life, despite the resistance of the old 'elites,' I guar-
> antee you this.
>
> [Я уважаю мнение украинцев, в течение месяцев мы слушаем
> предложения по реформам. Однако на митинге относительно
> закона о земле звучат не голоса фермеров, а политические
> лозунги. Мы прислушиваемся к людям. И именно так Украина
> будет двигаться к лучшей жизни, несмотря на сопротивление
> старых "элит". Это я вам гарантирую].

(Focus, 2019)

What is astonishing in this construction is Zelensky's refusal to accept
the obvious: Most Ukrainians have always been against land sales, and
the protesting farmers were representing this popular opinion. "Not the
voices of the farmers, but political slogans"—in the clearest possible
terms, this presidential claim reflected Zelensky's antipathy toward the
political, which he imagined exclusively in negative terms—as a performance staged by "old politicians" trying to prevent him from "moving
Ukraine to a better life."

From the discursive constructions of the "servants," the "good life" promised by Zelensky appeared inconceivable without land sales. In their collective view, the permission to sell land would serve as a magic carpet that would bring Ukrainians:

- The restoration of justice: "The law reform is not about land sale—it is about the restoration of justice" [земельная реформа—это не о распродаже земли, это о восстановлении справедливости]. (Honcharuk, 2019b)
- The restoration of law and order: "Deregulation, anti-raiding, transparency, protection of the rights of the landowner..." [Дерегуляция, анти-рейдерство, прозрачность, защита прав собственника земли...]. (Mylovanov, 2019c)
- Economic development: "[It] will give impetus to economic development, farming, agriculture in Ukraine" [Який дасть поштовх розвитку економіки, фермерству, аграрному комплексу в Україні]. (Shmyhal, 2020, 26:31–27:24)
- Economic growth: "We need a reform that will maximize economic growth" [Нам нужна та реформа, которая даст максимальный экономический рост]. (Mylovanov, 2019a)
- Enrichment for the people: "The price of land will increase, and people will become richer" [Ціна на землю збільшиться і люди стануть багатше]. (Mylovanov, 2019b)
- Democracy: "I also [like Margaret Thatcher] believe in a democracy based on property...Just as we are fighting sacredly for the right of citizens to dispose of their vote, we must give them the opportunity to dispose of their land" [Я теж вірю у демократію, засновану на власності. Так само, як ми свято боремося за право громадян розпоряджатися своїм голосом, ми маємо дати їм можливість розпоряджатися своєю землею]. (Mylovanov, 2019d)

Later, with the advent of the novel coronavirus and the economic deterioration associated with it, a final argument was deployed: The opening of the land market was necessary not only for saving the economy of Ukraine, but to save Ukraine itself. On March 29, 2020, on the eve of the adoption of the new law, Zelensky addressed the nation by outlining the situation as a matter of life and death:

Our country is off the road due to the coronavirus and has two paths. The first is the adoption of two vital laws. We will then receive support from our international financial partners of at least $10 billion. This is needed to stabilize the country's economy and overcome the crisis. Otherwise, the second way. This is a failure of these laws. After this—the decline of the economy and even the threat of default.

[Наша країна через коронавірус фактично опинилася на роздоріжжі і має два шляхи. Перше. Це ухвалення двох життєво важливих законів. Після цього ми отримаємо пидтримку від наших міжнародних фінансових партнерів у розмірі щонайменше 10 млрд доларів США. Це потрібно для стабілізації економіки країни та подолання кризи. Інакше другий шлях. Це провал цих законів. Після—занепад економіки і навіть загроза дефолту].

(Zelensky, 2020, 3:40–4:16)

Concluding his speech, Zelensky addressed the "servants," many of whom, under pressure from their constituents, hesitated to vote for the law:

Dear People's Deputies. All the responsibility tomorrow falls on your shoulders. Tomorrow, the people of Ukraine will clearly see whether you are ready to defend their interests. And, although tomorrow you will all be wearing masks, people will understand who is who. Society will understand whether you are servants of the people or servants of other people's interests. Realize your responsibility. Be aware of the possible consequences for each of you. Choose the right path tomorrow. You were elected by the people of Ukraine. Now it is your turn to choose the people of Ukraine.

[Шановні народні депутати. Вся відповідальність завтра лягає на ваші плечі. Завтра народ України чітко побачить, чи готові ви захищати його інтереси. І хоча завтра ви всі будете в масках, людям стане зрозуміло, хто є хто. Суспільство зрозуміє, ви слуги народу, чи прислужники чужих інтересів. Усвідомте свою відповідальність. Усвідомте можливі наслідки для кожного з вас. Оберіть завтра правильний шлях. Вас обрав народ України. Тепер ваша черга обрати народ України].

(Zelensky, 2020, 3:40–5:18)

Astonishing as it may sound, this excerpt clearly testifies that, despite most Ukrainians opposing land sales, Zelensky and those around him expressed absolute confidence that the reform was in the people's best interests. In their representation, there was no alternative to the land market, which, as the discursive constructions of the "servants" demonstrate, was linked inextricably to the following signifiers, all united equivalentially: the people's interests—democracy—justice—law and order—economic growth—prosperity—progress—Westernization—civilization. Apparently, in the eyes of Zelensky and his allies, the masses of manipulated Ukrainians simply did not realize what was best for them. It was the "white man's burden" of Zelensky's progressive team to enlighten the "savages" who stubbornly refused to be "civilized." These "barbarians," however, have turned out to be completely powerless to resist the onslaught of the neoliberal machine of the "servants."

Moralizing the Political

As is evident from the examples discussed in this chapter, Zelensky and his "servants" depoliticized the process of the adoption of the land reform by avoiding political negotiations under the premise that there was nobody to negotiate with on the issue: The opposition was portrayed as outdated, corrupted, and immoral; people opposing the reform as manipulated. Measured on the civilizational scale of progressive development, both the opposition and those who fell victim to its manipulations appeared as "barbarians" unable to recognize the high civilizational aspirations of the reformers. It is exactly this vision that has allowed Zelensky to ignore millions of people who opposed his reforms. In this sense, he has turned out to be no better than his predecessor Poroshenko, who, along with other Maidan leaders, ignored the millions of anti-Maidan Ukrainians because he perceived them as historical "ignoramuses."

People needed to be "corrected" and "old politicians" should be removed from the political field—this approach stemmed logically from such a vision of historical progress pushed forward by its avant-garde. As a result of this historical imaginary, the opponents of the reform had come to be imagined not as adversaries striving to organize the common symbolic space in a different way, but as enemies existing outside of the symbolic space shared by progressive "servants." The latter did not see the difference between themselves and their opponents positively, as a condition of possibility for the democratization of Ukrainian society; rather, they treated it in exclusively negative terms—as an abnormal historical condition in need of correction or eradication.

In "servant" articulations, the empty signifier "Soviet"/"sovok" has been linked primarily to a "lack of freedom" associated with people being unable to sell their land. The collective "sovok," standing in opposition to land sales, came to denote an evil that hampered free development, innovation, and the spontaneous course of history. In line with the classic neoliberal belief that justice is not about equal distribution but about universal rules common for all, the "servants" have remained deaf to the concerns of those warning that many Ukrainians will lose their resources for survival amid the market forces unleashed by the new law on selling land. "Sovki," "slaves," "modernization's losers," and the like will, if supported by state, slow down the advance of civilization—this has been a hidden message of the "servants" euphemized by their rhetoric of historical progress.

The collective "sovok" has been denounced so vehemently by the "servants" precisely for its rejection of the pure market, in which the fittest survive and catalyze progress while the weak and unfit (modernization's losers) are left behind. This dark side of the modernization story has been highlighted by the "servants" extremely rarely; only in occasional, subconscious slips has it been revealed, as in the case of the "servant" Galina Tretyakova who blurted out that the children of those dependent on welfare appear to be of "very low quality" [дуже низької якості] (Tretyakova, 2020, 00:08–00:11). Perfectly in line with the social Darwinism underlying some versions of neoliberal thinking (Leyva, 2009), the implication of this argument was that the state should abandon welfare so that such "low-quality" children could not be born. Because such sentiments cause backlash and resentment, they are rarely vocalized. The bitter dish of neoliberalization has been served with the sweet sauce of "civilization" and "prosperity for all."

The "servants" have never clearly articulated that traditional morality, which prescribes taking care of the weak, should be abandoned for the sake of neoliberal progress. They euphemized this idea by attacking the USSR, but the real target of their attack—the "sovok" ambition to eradicate inequality—was hidden under the rhetoric of attacking Soviet totalitarianism. In their discursive constructions, "lack of freedom" came to be a substitute for "equality": The link between "sovok" and "lack of freedom" was strengthened, while the link between "sovok" and "equality" was made invisible. This kind of euphemism allowed the "servants" to pretend they were attacking not equality, but totalitarianism.

This is why the dismantling of society through the privatization of all public services and goods has moved forward under the premise of a necessary dismantling of the totalitarian Soviet legacy; and this is why all oppositional attempts to defend society through preserving land—"the fundamental national wealth," as the Constitution of Ukraine defines it—have been perceived by the "servants" as attempts to preserve the "sovok." One would infer from the discursive constructions of the "servants" that no alternative society could exist—it is only their way or a return to the Soviet past. Seen this way, otherwise inconceivable interpretations by "servants" who take people's nostalgia for the welfare state as a sign of outdatedness, slavishness, uselessness, amorality, totalitarianism, and so forth begins to make sense. Whatever remains from the Soviet welfare legacy—such as free education, free health care, free housing—is attacked in the name of civilization and freedom, where the latter is interpreted in extremely narrow terms—predominantly, as the freedom to buy and sell. Calls for equality and inclusion come to be perceived as tyrannical; freedom comes to be associated exclusively with neoliberalism.

Notes

1 Oleksiy Honcharuk (born July 7, 1984) has master's degrees in law and public administration. Before starting his political career, he worked as a junior lawyer for the Horodnyansky food products plant, and later as a lawyer in the investment company PRIOR-Invest. Since 2015, Honcharuk has headed the Better Regulation Delivery Office (BRDO), which is funded by the European Union (112 Ukraine, 2019).

2 There are different views as to whether the "servants" actually lack competence at managing a real economy, or if they are intentionally seeking to deindustrialize Ukraine (see, for example, Kushch, 2021).

3 Genrikh Yagoda, Nikolai Yezhov, and Lavrentiy Beria were the leaders of the People's Commissariat of Internal Affairs, infamously known as the NKVD. Yagoda was one of the organizers of the dispossession of peasants in Ukraine, Russia, and Kazakhstan in the 1930s; under his leadership, the General Directorate of Forced Labor Camps (GULag) was organized. Yezhov acted as one of the organizers of the mass repressions of 1937–1938. Under the leadership of Beria, a mass deportation was carried out from Belarus and Ukraine as well as the Baltic states in 1939–1940. In 1944, Beria led the operations to deport Chechens, Ingush, Karachais, Kalmyks, Tatars and other peoples from the Caucasian republics and Crimea.

References

112 Ukraine. (2019, August 30). New Prime Minister of Ukraine: Who Is he? Retrieved from https://112.international/ukraine-top-news/new-prime-minister-of-ukraine-who-is-he-43067.html

Arakhamia, D. (2020, February 7). "Батькивщина"—это маленький комар ["Fatherland" is a little Insect]. *YouTube*. Retrieved from https://www.youtube.com/watch?v=wm7E2sB6Vjs

BNE Intellinews. (2020, December 25). The decline of Ukraine's industrial output slowed to 0.3% y/y in November. Retrieved from https://intellinews.com/the-decline-of-ukraine-s-industrial-output-slowed-to-0-3-y-y-in-november-199314/?source=ukraine

Constitution. (1996). Constitution of Ukraine. Retrieved from https://www.refworld.org/pdfid/44a280124.pdf

Dubilet, D. (2019, November 2013). The moratorium on the land sale. *YouTube*. Retrieved from https://www.facebook.com/dubilet/posts/10157910625633552

Focus. (2019, December 17). Зеленский осудил столкновения од Радой [Zelensky condemned clashes near Rada]. Retrieved from https://focus.ua/ukraine/446692zelenskii_osudil_stolknoveniia_pod_radoi_eto_byli_ne_golosa_fermerov

Hartley, J. (1992). *The politics of pictures: The creation of the public in the age of popular media*. London & New York: Routledge.

Honcharuk, O. (2019a, September 19). Рынок земли в Украине уже есть давно, только он "серый" [The land market in Ukraine has been around for a long time, only it is "gray"] *YouTube*. Retrieved from https://www.youtube.com/watch?v=TeG2ofTmH6k

Honcharuk, O. (2019b, November 13). Не можем удовлетворить всех, будем балансировать [We cannot satisfy everyone, we will balance]. *Economy Pravda*. Retrieved from https://www.epravda.com.ua/rus/news/2019/11/13/653660

Kushch, A. (2021, June 10). Рынок земли—одна из самых больших ошибок нынешней власти [The land market is one of the biggest mistakes of the current government]. YouTube. Retrieved from https://www.youtube.com/watch?v=YTOs7ThtLFo

Kvitka, V. (2019, November 13). Битва за Сталинград начинается [A battle for Stalingrad begins. *Strana.UA]*. Retrieved from https://strana.ua/articles/private-life/233247-hlava-fraktsii-sn-david-arakhamija-razoslal-sms-instruktsiju-zedeputatam-bitva-za-stalinhradnachinaetsja.html

Laclau, E., & Mouffe, C. (1985). *Hegemony and socialist strategy: Towards a radical democratic politics*. London: Verso.

Leyva, R. (2009). No child left behind: A neoliberal repackaging of social Darwinism. *Journal for Critical Education Policy Studies*, 7(1), 364–381.

Mouffe, C. (2005). *On the political*. London: Routledge.

Mylovanov, T. (2019a, September 8). Не нужно бороться с бизнес-моделями компаний [There is no need to fight against the business models of companies]. *HB*. Retrieved from https://nv.ua/biz/economics/ministr-ekonomiki-milovanov-intervyu-novosti-ukrainy-50041337.html

Mylovanov, T. (2019b, October 7). Що пропонується в реформі про землю? [What does the land reform offer?] *Facebook*. Retrieved from https://www.facebook.com/permalink.php?story_fbid=147605988589652 2&id=100004775745586

Mylovanov, T. (2019c, November 13). Сегодня исторический день [Today is a historic day]. *Interfax-Ukraine*. Retrieved from https://interfax.com.ua/news/economic/624334.html

Mylovanov, T. (2019d, November 13). Землевладелец должен чувствовать себя владельцем, а не крепостным [The landowner should feel like an owner, not a serf]. *BizLiga*. Retrieved from https://biz.liga.net/ekonomika/prodovolstvie/opinion/zemlevladelets-doljen-chuvstvovat-sebya-vladeltsem-a-ne-krepostnym

Poturaev, M. (2019, November 13). Мы сведем счеты с Лениным и Сталиным [We will settle scores with Lenin and Stalin]. *YouTube*. Retrieved from https://www.youtube.com/watch?v=OS0wGnLhGXs.

Shmyhal, D. (2020, March 5). Political talk-show "The Right to Power." *YouTube*. Retrieved from https://www.youtube.com/watch?v=ovI-PvUNGoA

Tretyakova, G. (2020, June 24). Безработные рожают детей низкого качества [Unemployed people give birth to inferior children]. *YouTube*. Retrieved from https://www.youtube.com/watch?v=MxhWCD1VJeQ

World Bank. (n/d). GDP growth (% annual)—Ukraine. Retrieved from https://data.worldbank.org/indicator/NY.GDP.MKTP.KD.ZG?locations=UA

Zelensky, V. (2019a, September 19). Володимир Зеленський на конференції, присвяченій земельній реформі [Volodymyr Zelensky at the conference on land administration reform]. *YouTube*. https://www.youtube.com/watch?v=bclyrDlbhCM&t=442s

Zelensky, V. (2019b, November 11). Срочное обращение президента Зеленского [An urgent address of President Zelensky]. *YouTube*. Retrieved from https://www.youtube.com/watch?v=tE_V6PxPYA8

Zelensky, V. (2020, March 29). Обращение Зеленского от 29 марта [Zelensky's address of March 29]. *YouTube*. Retrieved from https://www.youtube.com/watch?v=QqrdJKw_HBw

7 The Post-Political Tyranny of the Integral

Does Reality Exist?

Does not the whole story of Zelensky's ascent to power through his fictional character on *Servant of the People* provide a perfect illustration of Jean Baudrillard's (2005) "integral universe" in which "reality is disappearing at the hands of the cinema and the cinema is disappearing at the hands of reality" (p. 125), and where "there are no actors or spectators anymore" (p. 135)? Is this not a game "on the fringes of the real and its disappearance" (Baudrillard, 2005, p. 69) in which "we are all immersed in the same reality, in the same revolving responsibility, in a single destiny that is merely the fulfilment of a collective desire" (Baudrillard, 2005, p. 135)? These questions have been raised on Ukraine's political programs that discussed Zelensky's route to the presidency and whose analysts have been asking each other: "Is this reality? Or another joke? Is this still a performance? Are we already in a simulacrum?" (Channel 5, 2021). Here is an interesting excerpt along these lines from a TV program:

KARASYOV: This is a cinematic reality that gave Zelensky the opportunity to go to the second round. To win the first round. Because what is a TV show? It is not Zelensky who promises—Holoborodko promises... The actor promises! The character promises!

[Это кинематографическая реальность, которая дала возможность Зеленскому выйти по второй тур. Победить в первом туре. Потому что что такое кино? Обещает же не Зеленский – обещает Голобородько... Актер обещает! Персонаж обещает!]

HOST: Then, against whom will the impeachment be—against Zelensky or Holoborodko—if anything happens?

DOI: 10.4324/9781003228493-8

[Ну так а проти кого буде імпічмент, проти Зеленського чи Голобородька, у разі чого?]

(Karasyov, 2019, 10:43–11:13)

Although this was not a serious question, it drew a big laugh in the studio because it evoked the country's experience of blurred realities, which was also in line with what Baudrillard observed. "'Does reality exist? Are we in a real world?'—this is the leitmotiv of our entire present culture," he claimed more than a decade before Zelensky's triumph (Baudrillard, 2005, p. 26).

In Zelensky's case, the line separating the real from the virtual was blurred from the very beginning; it was not exactly clear where the performance ended and democratic deliberation began, or what political course would actually be taken. Election promises were euphemized to the point of the unreal, but no one could be held accountable or even take responsibility for this because the promises had been made within a fictional TV series. Everything turned out to be simulacrum: Zelensky's election pledges performed by Holoborodko, his "party," the "democratic" procedure of adopting laws through a party machine created exclusively for this purpose, the "people's needs" as constructed by Zelensky, and so forth. Because the virtual and the real blurred, Ukrainians found themselves in a grey zone with no boundaries, no truth, and no lies—a zone that "devours both actors and counteractors in its huge belly and even feeds off resistance: it cuts the ground from under the feet of resisters by eliminating the principle of opposition" (Beck, 2007, p. 290). The dismantling of the political—a logical outcome of the dismantling of the principle of opposition—is one of the main features of Zelensky's neoliberal authoritarianism that has been forged on the fringes of the virtual and the real.

Ignoring the tremendous complexity of the real, Zelensky in his show created a phantom world of virtual reality—an "integral," flawless universe with "all psychological or emotional pathology removed" (Baudrillard, 2005, p. 28). Following a utopian "impulse to resolve the ambivalence of good and evil and jump over one's shadow into absolute positivity" (Baudrillard, 2005, p. 51), Zelensky created "the absurdity of a total truth from which falsehood is lacking—that of absolute good from which evil is lacking, of the positive from which the negative is lacking" (Baudrillard, 2005, p. 34). The utopia of absolute positivity, created by Zelensky in the show, removed all "pathology": oligarchs, corrupted politicians, enemies, conflicts, etc. All complexities were eliminated; all contradictions removed; all "others" abolished.

Holoborodko's perfect society—an artificial paradise with ideal living conditions—was sterile, not infected with politics. This integral utopia was totally transparent and liberated from any evil force, like a genetically engineered social heaven. Transferred into absolute positivity, the real was totalized and virtualized. At the cost of an extraordinary simplification, the entire system of integral power, created by Zelensky, has been pushing the real toward totality and unification—a totalitarian dream.

There is no political struggle in Holoborodko's flawless society; everything is perfected by the will of an "enlightened" ruler and the non-corrupted officials around him. In this "radiant universe ready to pass over into the next world" (Baudrillard, 2005, p. 147), society is already saved, with nothing lacking in either politics or democracy. There is not even a need for representation—"the principle of representation itself disappears beneath the calculation" (p. 41). Indeed, did the party of "servants"—the product forged on the fringes of the virtual and the real—represent those who voted it into power? Within the coordinates of the flawless integral utopia created by Zelensky, this question appears senseless. As Baudrillard's (2005) theory maintains, and as the analysis in this book suggests, "there is no longer ultimately any possible representation" (p. 97). What appears instead is the integral calculus of reality. Everybody is set to zero in the name of integral happiness.

The banality of the show has merged with the banality of reality—the product of Zelensky's virtual world. The real has immersed itself in the digital, and the digital in the real. Zelensky's party machine has become the virtual reality of his show—"an ectoplasm of the screen," as Baudrillard (2005, p. 81) put it. The distinction between man and machine has been erased, and machines have appeared on both sides of the interface. After all, "machines produce only machines," as Baudrillard (2005, p. 80) observed—all that can come out of the digital world is a machine product.

But the problem with this integral universe created by Zelensky is that Ukrainians took the virtual for the real and applied the categories of the latter to the former, while "the specificity of the Virtual is that it constitutes an event in the real against the real and throws into question all these categories of the real, the social, the political" (Baudrillard, 2005, p. 83). When the virtual is confused for the real, politics disappear—only virtuality remains. Zelensky's integral creation could not create democracy; it could only produce its simulation. Under such circumstances, public opinion has only virtual significance—Ukrainians seem to have finally realized this after the launch of the land reform against their will. Instead of the accession of all Ukrainians to political participation, the integral machine created by Zelensky only strengthened the privileged status of elites; in the virtual world of simulacra invented by the comedian in a playful gesture, ordinary Ukrainians can no longer find their place. The comedian's integral creation has delivered Ukrainians from the boring and troublesome responsibility of sharing power. In the absence of any representativeness or credibility, Zelensky's party machine has been making its way toward neoliberal paradise despite people's disapprobation.

Because the power bulldozer created by Zelensky has little to do with political representation, public opinion has been disregarded completely. By ignoring people's resistance to land sale, the machine demonstrated their political insignificance—their actual non-existence. This is the crux of the issue. Power can only be challenged if it derives its sovereignty from representation. The lack of representation makes power uncontrolled and cruel—a product of the integral times, when power is exercised "in the pure state with no concern for sovereignty or representation" (Baudrillard, 2005, p. 120).

An integral system, liberated from representation and opposition, has established a monopoly over the rules by uniting equivalentially Westernization, evolutionism, neoliberalization, and progress, thus setting the ultimate limits of the thinkable, the finality of imagination. Characterized by extreme banality, Zelensky's integral creation has presented neoliberalization as progressive development and market fundamentalism as a historical advance. Reducing a "complex and differentiated global political economy to a race for economic and political advance" (Ferguson, 1999, p. 16), its narrative has not been about neoliberal transformations—the dismantling of the social and the debilitation of the political—but about progress. According to this story line, simplified to the extreme, Ukraine has been moving along the avenue leading to "civilization," "Westernization," and "modernization."

Social perfection has come to be imagined exclusively in terms of unification modeled according to "Western standards" and technical advance. It is pertinent to recall here Zelensky's dream about "the reduction of all the functions of the state to the size of a smartphone" [зведення всього функціоналу держави до розмірів смартфону] (Zelensky, 2019). Importantly, these "progressive" "civilizational" aspirations have been devoid of any claim to cultural specificity or originality of thought. "To Westernize," "to be like they are," "to reach their level," "to transform ourselves into them," "to become different and to scramble out of our skins"—these mantras, known from *perestroika* times, delimited the final frontier of the thinkable for the "servants."

Even if, following postmodern critical thinkers, we assume that the whole intellectual project of the Enlightenment was rather naïve in its incapability "of thinking beyond an ideal version of man" (Baudrillard, 2005, p. 141), Zelensky's version of historical progressivism is the utmost emasculation of Enlightenment ideas—a "second-hand" appropriation of them. It is not about the unlimited progress of the human spirit, but about growth limited by preestablished frontiers—not an unleashing of human creativity, but rather a leashing of it with preestablished standards of Westernization, imagined in extremely simplified neoliberal terms. This is what Baudrillard (2005) called "the fall of imagination" (p. 70)—the lack of any necessity to think creatively, as the track has already been trodden: the track of progressive linear development with the established horizon of standardized improvement, where good is measured in terms of economic liberalization and technical mastery and where the "state in a smartphone" is seen as "the kingdom of ends." The complexity of the political has been replaced by the simplest possible solution: the appropriation of Western modernity (imagined in the primitive terms of a linear economic advance) with ready-made neoliberal fixes for all problems. It is this extreme limitation of the imaginary that explains the utter naivete in Zelensky's view of current events and his inability to realize the complexities of global issues in all their economic, political, and social dimensions.

There Is No Alternative to the Integral

As long ago as 1985, Laclau and Mouffe theorized that a truly democratic condition could be achieved only if the link between the evolutionist paradigm and democratic theorization were broken. According to Laclau and Mouffe (1985), it is only through this radical break that any totalizing ideology, which transforms a conjunctural state of affairs into a historical necessity, can be deconstructed. This break would make it possible to see that any given historical conjuncture is not the natural order of things, but rather the expression of certain power configurations; it would also enable the imagining of alternative ways to organize the social, which could foreground unexpected historical turns.

To open up the imagination toward new democratic possibilities, we need to "withdraw the category of 'necessity' to the horizon of the social," Laclau and Mouffe (1985, p. 13) argued, because neither a fixed path of linear development nor the application of "inexorable laws" for social transformation are compatible with open democratic imagination. The logic of necessity operates through fixed meanings and limitations that restrain the work of the symbolic; it creates "totalizing contexts which fix a priori the meaning of every event" (Laclau & Mouffe, 1985, p. 34). To avoid totalization, therefore, we need to avoid thinking in terms of "normal" stages of historical development and "normal" models of historical change.

In Laclau and Mouffe's view, authoritarian methods of government are intrinsically connected to the evolutionary imagination that presents historical conjuncture as inevitable historical necessity. Anti-democratic authoritarian tendencies inherent in "progressive" historical endeavors stem from "essentialist apriorism, the conviction that the social is sutured at some point, from which it is possible to fix the meaning of any event independently of any articulatory practice" (Laclau & Mouffe, 1985, p. 176). It is this "essentialist apriorism" that, in the view of Laclau and Mouffe, "galvanized the political imagination" of Jacobin-style revolutionaries whose thinking is incompatible with democratic government. According to Laclau and Mouffe (1985),

> Sticking to the evolutionary paradigm of democratic theorizing will inevitably lead to polarizing political effects since the progressive imaginary presupposes the existence of strict dividing lines between "progressive" and "regressive" forces of history with "military relations" between them.
>
> (p. 70)

In Laclau and Mouffe's view, non-military relations—that is, inclusive/pluralistic democratic politics—can only come to life if there are no rigid boundaries between identities and if the category of "objective interest" from a predetermined historical agent is abandoned, since it only holds meaning within an eschatological conception of history.

The basic precondition for a radically libertarian conception of politics is the refusal to dominate—intellectually or politically. It is this precondition that is unachievable if the project of liberation is conceived in unidirectional evolutionary terms, as a movement toward a "more advanced" societal condition under the domination of self-proclaimed "progressive forces of history." In Laclau and Mouffe's view,

> This point is decisive: there is no radical and plural democracy without renouncing the discourse of the universal and its implicit assumption of a privileged point of access to 'the truth', which can be reached only by a limited number of subjects.
>
> (Laclau & Mouffe, 1985, pp. 191–192)

To be inclusively democratic, the discourse of a universal history should be replaced with the discourse of a variety of historical projects articulated by "a polyphony of voices, each of which constructs its own irreducible discursive identity," Laclau and Mouffe assert (1985, p. 191).

In her later works, Mouffe developed these ideas further, arguing that "we should stop presenting the institutions of liberal western societies as the solution that other people will necessarily adopt when they cease to be 'irrational' and become 'modern'" (Mouffe, 2009, p. 65). Pluralist democracy should recognize that there cannot be one single project suitable for governing different societies: This question cannot be conceived in singular and universal terms. The world should be conceived as a "pluri-verse," which acknowledges "a plurality of regional poles, organized according to different economic and political models without a central authority" (Mouffe, 2013, p. 22) and a multiplicity of interpretations of "democracy."

In Mouffe's (2013) view, democracy, understood as rule by the people, "can take a variety of forms, according to the different modes of inscription of the democratic ideal in the variety of contexts" (p. 29). The possibility of interpreting "democracy" in a variety of ways stems from the pluralism of cultures, forms of life, and different understandings of "human dignity." Rather than insisting on the path followed by the West as the only possible and legitimate one, we should acknowledge that "non-Western societies can follow different trajectories according to the specificity of their cultural traditions and religions," as Mouffe claims (2013, p. 35). Any political project on a global scale should be conceived with an open-ended horizon that allows for unrestricted possibilities of hegemonic articulations.

According to Mouffe, only through this radicalization of the global democratic imaginary can we challenge the "there is no alternative" dogma of neoliberalism, which transforms a contingent historical articulation from a specific cultural context into a historical necessity. To subvert the neoliberal hegemony that arrests imagination, she argues, one needs to "question the dominant narrative about the superiority of the Western form of development" (Mouffe, 2013, p. 36), "challenge the dangerous thesis that democratization requires Westernization" (Mouffe, 2013, p. 40), and deconstruct the "naturalness" of the universality of the Western developmental path:

> Such a hegemony is the result of a discursive construction that articulates in a very specific manner a manifold of practices, discourses and language games of a very diverse nature. If it can be perceived as the natural consequence of technological progress, it

is because, through a process of sedimentation, the political origin of these contingent practices has been erased; they have become naturalized, and the forms of identification that they have produced have crystallized in identities which are taken for granted.

(Mouffe, 2009, p. 89)

This is why, according to Mouffe, neoliberal transfromations appear as a natural historical process—"as a fate that we have to accept because 'there is no alternative'" (Mouffe, 2013, p. 89).

This is exactly what we observe in the case of Zelensky's project. Through his utopia of absolute positivity—an "integral," flawless universe existing without pathology, complexity, or contradictions—Zelensky has created a perfectly sterile integral space not infected with politics and liberated from political antagonisms. In line with Mouffe's (2005) observation regarding "the post-political Zeitgeist" where "the political is played out in the moral register" (p. 4), the political contestation of alternative views has been substituted with the moralism of the belief in neoliberal salvation, presented as a historical inevitability and advancement.

The forces that ended up in opposition to neoliberal transfromations have been attacked not politically (based on opposing opinions) but morally (based on the accusation of "hampering historical progress"). "In place of a struggle of 'right and left,' we are faced with a struggle between 'right and wrong'" (Mouffe, 2005, p. 4)—this has been the essence of "politics" within Zelensky's integral project. While the "servants" have been vehemently attacking the Soviet project, they have done so not on ideological but on moral grounds. Presenting linear development as natural, universally legitimate, and—most importantly—morally superior, Zelensky's power machine has fostered a Jacobin revolutionary imaginary incompatible with democratic governance. It has reduced the polyphony of voices opposing neoliberalization to the uniformity of a "there is no alternative" stance.

References

Baudrillard, J. (2005). *The intelligence of evil*. New York: Berg.

Beck, U. (2007). *Power in the global age: A new global political economy*. Cambridge: Polity Press.

Channel 5. (2021, February 3). Это реальность, или мы уже в симуляции? [Is this reality or are we already in a simulacrum?] *Channel 5*. Retrieved from https://www.5.ua/ru/obshchestvo/eto-realnost-yly-mi-uzhe-v-symuliatsyy-sotssety-vzorvalys-shutkamy-yz-za-blokyrovky-newsone-112-y-zik-235815.html

Ferguson, J. (1999). *Expectations of modernity: Myths and meanings of urban life on the Zambian Copperbelt.* Berkeley: University of California Press.

Karasyov, V. (2019, April 10). Вадим Карасев на 112 [Vadim Karasyov na 112]. *YouTube.* Retrieved from https://www.youtube.com/watch?v=L6g443XgNPw

Laclau, E., & Mouffe, C. (1985). *Hegemony and socialist strategy: Towards a radical democratic politics.* London: Verso.

Mouffe, C. (2005). *On the political.* London: Routledge.

Mouffe, C. (2009). *The democratic paradox.* New York: Verso.

Mouffe, C. (2013). *Agonistics: Thinking the world politically.* New York: Verso.

Zelensky, V. (2019, May 23). Я мрію про державу у смартфоні [I dream about a smartphone State]. *President of Ukraine Official Website.* Retrieved from https://www.president.gov.ua/news/ya-mriyu-pro-derzhavu-u-smartfoni-volodimir-zelenskij-55585

8   Democracy-to-Come
A Perpetual Promise

Dismantling the Political

As outlined in Chapter 1, by means of his policy of *glasnost*, Gorbachev consciously unleashed the democratic energy emanating from the people so as to suppress opposition to his reforms aimed at "updating socialism." The release of this energy brought unpredicted results: Gorbachev was removed from power and his socialist agenda was derailed, leaving unfulfilled all the best intentions to create a society in which social justice, equality, and prosperity would reign. Zelensky (or those surrounding him—see below) seem(s) to understand that unconstrained democracy can bring unexpected outcomes—after all, Zelensky himself came to power on a wave of popular love that may be characterized as irrational. It is quite possible, therefore, that keeping democratic energies leashed by means of "servants'" party machine was a conscious desire to protect Zelensky's unpopular reforms from "the abuses of democracy," to put it in Friedrich Hayek's words (Farrant et al., 2012, p. 513).

To be sure, the post-Soviet Ukraine before Zelensky was also imperfect in terms of its democratic condition. This was evident in the unequal access to economic and political resources—the oligarchic legacy of the 1990s—or in election manipulations, which came to be the main reason for the Orange Revolution of 2004.[1] What Zelensky has brought to this tradition of excluding the people from sociopolitical processes is the sophistication of simulacra. He came to power through an ostensibly democratic procedure—free elections. No manipulation of the vote count such as occurred in the case of Yanukovych in 2004 was necessary since most Ukrainians supported Zelensky. The trick required finesse on a level Yanukovych never would have imagined: The voters simply did not know what they were voting for. But the result was the same—the exhaustion of democracy, as well as people's trust in it.

DOI: 10.4324/9781003228493-9

Of course, a perfectly democratic condition measured in terms of political equality is an unachievable dream in any capitalist society. As Wendy Brown (2018) put it, "democratic capitalism is also an oxymoron... Capitalism can be modulated in more or less democratic directions, and states can do more or less to nurture or quash the political equality on which democracy depends" (pp. 25–26). The direction chosen by Zelensky has put the country squarely on a "less democratic" path. To achieve a better democratic condition, the government would need to adopt very specific policies aimed at reducing the inequalities among citizens in terms of their ability to influence political decisions. In contrast, Zelensky has been acting to create power mechanisms that prevent the people from influencing political decisions.

The principle of equality—the main principle of democratic government—has been undermined by Zelensky at every turn. The equal right of every citizen to speak and be heard on matters of public policy was violated with the closure of oppositional TV channels, which had been expressing the views of a growing number of Ukrainians unsatisfied with Zelensky's rule. The equality of citizens under the law was violated when the NSDC initiated extrajudicial reprisals through the imposition of sanctions. Equality in terms of opportunities to serve in political office was violated when Zelensky's friends assumed public positions, and so on.

Zelensky's power machine managed to limit and contain the political by sapping its democratic energies and thus de-democratizing it. Politics has been reduced to authoritarian administration, and technocratic solutions have come to replace democratic deliberation that involved the contestation of ideas, arguments, and the working out of political decisions for the public good. Instead, what has been put into motion— as is necessary for the implementation of neoliberal reforms—is a depoliticized and technocratic state machine, safeguarded from "democratic excesses" of all sorts. In this sense, Zelensky's tendency to see oppositional movements as staged by oligarchs, rather than as genuine manifestations of discontentment among the people, is revealing. This is how he imagines democratic processes—as staged, orchestrated, and controlled.

There is a significant difference between the version of a neoliberal state designed by Zelensky and the one envisioned by Soviet neoliberals of the early 1990s. For the latter, the invisible hand of the market was assumed to put things in order by itself; but for Zelensky, the state has been deemed necessary to create all the necessary conditions for neoliberal governance. His design for such a state presupposes its safeguarding from the demands of the masses. By means of his parliamentary machine, he has been able to find a new and unconventional solution to the old problem haunting the greatest neoliberal minds: how "to inoculate capitalism against the threat of democracy, to create a framework to contain often-irrational human behavior" (Slobodian, 2020, p. 2). Seen this way, Zelensky's project (or somebody else's project called by his name) does not appear as funny and naïve as it seemed at first glance. The attempts of his team to create an authoritarian state liberated from "democratic excesses" is in line with classic neoliberal thought, rejecting full-fledged democratic governance and the expansive notion of the political in which such governance rests.

On the Shoulders of Neoliberal Giants

In his book *Globalists*, Slobodian (2020) challenges a widely shared assumption about neoliberals' ostensible belief in global laissez-faire, self-regulating markets, and shrunken states. In his account, "the neoliberal project focused on designing institutions—not to liberate markets but to encase them, to inoculate capitalism against the threats of democracy" (p. 2). According to Slobodian, thinking about how to safeguard the world economy (to insulate the market) from democratic pressures has been a general tendency among "ordoglobalists"—the term coined by Slobodian to designate the continental school of neoliberal thinking (Geneva School), which has been much more attentive to the issues of global governance than its Anglo-American counterparts.

In Slobodian's account, because democracy became an influential global factor only in the 20th century, the idea of "democracy constraint," which would have been unthinkable for classical liberals, came to distinguish the neoliberals of the post-war order, which was characterized by the ruin of empire, decolonization, and the emergence of new nation-states. "The confrontation with mass democracy was also at the heart of the century for neoliberals... [for whom]... [t]he tension was always between advocating democracy for peaceful change and condemning its capacity to upend order," Slobodian (2020, p. 14) claims. In other words, in Slobodian's view, neoliberals valued democratic governance as a means of peaceful organic change stemming from open competition and free innovation; therefore, democracy should not be destroyed—rather, it must be limited so as to prevent it from destroying itself.

Slobodian is in line with numerous other scholars who see the creation of supranational governing institutions such as the IMF, the World Bank, and the WTO, and international treaties such as NAFTA, as attempts to insulate markets from democratic pressures coming from sovereign nation-states (e.g., Babb, 2009; Chorev, 2005; Harmes, 2006). According to this outlook, the creation of a parallel global legal system, the spread of offshore tax havens, and the foundation of various other types of special economic zones are similar developments in one sense—they are all designed to safeguard capital from the risks of progressive taxation, equal redistribution, and other manifestations of the democratic ambition of achieving social equality. From this perspective, neoliberalism appears as a project aimed specifically at building institutions to protect markets from democratic interventions of all sorts—to find "a legal and institutional fix for the disruptive effects of democracy on market processes" (Slobodian, 2020, p. 11). What is essential in this view is that the neoliberal goal is not about liberating markets from the state and making them self-regulated or "disembedded," to use Polanyi's (2001) terms, but about protecting the market through the creation of a suitable legal-institutional framework while redesigning the state. It is assumed, in other words, that markets are not given from nature—they are constructed purposefully through the creation of extra-economic conditions.

It stems logically from such an understanding of neoliberalism that it should be suspicious not only about democracy but also about the strong sovereignty of nation-states. As Slobodian (2020) put it, "Ordoglobalism was haunted by two puzzles across the twentieth century: first, how to rely on democracy, given democracy's capacity to destroy itself; and second, how to rely on nations, given nationalism's capacity to 'disintegrate the world'" (p. 13). Nation-states, ordoglobalists believed, should be incorporated into the global institutional regime of safeguarding the free market; ideally, they should all be guarded by the same laws. In other words, "the excesses of sovereignty should be abolished," as Wilhelm Röpke put it (cited in Bonefeld, 2015, p. 868). Searching for an adequate balance between the global economic order and national political regimes so as to reconcile global dependency with national self-determination has been the main neoliberal problem of post-colonial times. The neoliberals of the Geneva School did not envisage the dissolution of nation-states; rather, they imagined structured relations between them and the global institutions of economic regulation, with the ability of supranational institutions to override national legislation threatening to violate the global rights of capital. Nation-states, this outlook holds, may be useful in terms of maintaining political legitimacy and stability. Global institutions should work with them to ensure the effective functioning of the global economic system. But if the latter is threatened by popular decisions, the supranational system must be able to override them.

To sum up, neoliberal thinking, at least in its "ordoglobal" version, is primarily about coming up with an institutional framework—encompassing both global and local power structures—to preempt national-democratic opposition to the development of free capitalist markets on a global scale in the form of demands for social justice understood as egalitarian redistribution. I find this insight very helpful to make sense of Zelensky's project. If evaluated from the ordoglobal perspective, his course of action appears logical and even successful: Having mobilized the democratic energy of the people through his populist *Servant of the People*'s real-virtual power machine, Zelensky was able to effectively curb it after winning the election.

"Servants" of Globalism

Democracy is about organizing political life in such a way so that the people can govern themselves. Zelensky's power machine has been designed such that people cannot do this. The future of Ukraine's agricultural land was decided without regard to the opinion of Ukrainians—a nod of approval from "Western partners" (a catchphrase used by Ukrainian neoliberal reformers) was enough to bring Ukrainian black soil under the hammer. The World Bank, the EBRD, the IMF, the G-7, neoliberal think-tanks, lobbying groups, financial speculators, etc.—all the advocates of neoliberal globalism have welcomed the Ukrainian land reform and pushed for the opening of the land market despite the mass disapproval of Ukrainians. Under pressure from global neoliberal institutions, in addition to the "excesses" of Ukraine's democratic condition, its "excess" national sovereignty has also been eliminated.

To be sure, Ukraine's incorporation into the global neoliberal network started long before Zelensky. It can be traced to the early 1990s, when the law On Foreign Investments and the decree On the Regime of Foreign Investment were adopted, which "provided state guarantee to foreign investors on investment return and protection from changes to investment and taxation legislation for ten years" (Yurchenko, 2018, p. 93). However, since global hegemony of capital cannot be guaranteed by mere market penetration of transnational capital into a client state, the whole process has been coordinated by global neoliberal institutions such as the IMF, the World Bank, the EBRD, etc. Ukrainian legislation has been subject to continual revision in accordance with the requirements of these and numerous other neoliberal guardians.

The complete story of Ukraine's neoliberal transformation is long and complex, but for the purposes of this book, suffice it to say that the process of establishing foreign control over Ukraine has intensified significantly since the 1990s. In the early years of Ukraine's independence, one could hardly imagine the country appointing foreign citizens to top ministerial posts—a development that became possible two decades later. It was after the victory of the Euromaidan that foreign presence in Ukrainian governmental structures started to be perceived as normal. Natalie Jaresko—a citizen of the US—was appointed Ukraine's Minister of Finance (2014–2016).[2] Aivaras Abromavičius—a citizen of Lithuania—became Ukraine's Minister of Economy and Trade (2014–2016)[3]; Alexander Kvitashvili—a citizen of Georgia—was the Minister of Healthcare (2014–2016)[4]; and Ulana Suprun—a citizen of the US—served as the acting Minister of Healthcare (2016–2019).[5] Other foreigners assumed offices of lower ranks (Tyshchuk, 2017). Some of them became Ukrainian citizens as soon as they occupied governmental positions; however, this does not negate the fact that their appointments resulted not from the will of Ukrainians but from the recommendations of the global institutional regime of safeguarding free market, as Slobodian might have called this.

Although there have been no foreign citizens serving as ministers in the two governments under Zelensky's presidency, his officials have been closely connected with global centers of neoliberal power (Vishnevsky, 2020). It is these people who have sought to reconcile global dependency with Ukraine's sovereign ambitions, working to strike a balance between the global economic order and Ukrainian sociopolitical realities. A leaked audio recording in which Prime Minister Honcharuk (2019–2020) discusses with his colleagues how to delude Zelensky is very interesting in this respect. Here is Honcharuk's direct speech:

> Zelensky has a very primitive, in this sense, simple understanding of economic processes. There is a balance of payments. The balance of payments has not improved much, and the hryvnia [UAH, Ukrainian currency] has strengthened a lot... He is looking for an answer to this question.

> [У Зеленского есть очень примитивное понимание экономических процессов. Есть платежный баланс. А они насильно укрепили. Он ищет ответ на этот вопрос. А у него нет ответа на этот вопрос].

> (Delo.ua, 2020)

Honcharuk instructs his colleagues on what they should tell Zelensky to persuade him that everything is under control and that the government's policy is for the benefit of Ukraine:

> He needs to explain the following: at the beginning of the year, the population did not believe in the hryvnia... Then a new strong president blah blah blah... The level of trust in the authorities is unprecedented. The hryvnia continues to strengthen.... We need to speak very convincingly.... Because until the president has an answer to this question in his head, he will have an empty space there, and crap about bonds will fly there. It only hits his head because there is a fog in it.

> [Ему нужно объяснить следующее: в начале года население не верило в гривню... Потом новый сильный президент бла-бла-бла... Уровень доверия беспрецедентный к власти. Гривня продолжает укрепляться... Будем говорить очень реалистично... Потому что пока у нас не будет у президента в голове ответа на этот вопрос — у него будет пустое место там. И к нему будет прилетать эта хрень на тему облигаций. Она попадает в голову только потому, что у него есть туман].
>
> (Delo.ua, 2020)

By "bonds," Honcharuk means government securities that, starting from December 2019, have been actively purchased by global financial speculators and, according to rumors, by Ukrainian officials connected with them. The great profitability of the bonds and rapid growth in demand for them boosted the exchange rate of the UAH against the USD and radically reduced the profits of Ukrainian exporters, which negatively influenced budget revenue. As a result, by the end of 2019, the government had to suspend most of its payments since there was not enough money in state coffers. To plug the growing public finance deficit, the government continued issuing the bonds, which strengthened the hryvnia even further, threatening the whole economic system (Kozak, 2020).

This is the essence of the story, which Honcharuk tried to hide by inventing a legend about people's trust in the hryvnia—a fairy tale concocted specifically for Zelensky. A nuance worth noting about this meeting, whose leaked audio caused a scandal, is that its participants included the country's Minister of Finance Oksana Markarova[6] and Minister of Economic Development, Trade and Agriculture Tymofiy Mylovanov[7]—two other key figures in the Ukrainian government (in addition to Honcharuk) connected with global neoliberal institutions (Vishnevsky, 2020).

This story is interesting because it clearly demonstrates how those surrounding Zelensky manipulates him to achieve their goals. Many experts believe that Zelensky's unshakable conviction that the opening of the land market will bring prosperity for all Ukrainians is a result of similar manipulations, when Zelensky's naivety in economic affairs is simply "used blindly," as Kushch put it:

> Zelensky in this case is simply being used blindly. His entourage has successfully persuaded him that he will go down in history as a great reformer—almost like Tsar Alexander II, the liberator, who abolished serfdom… He has been persuaded that this is his historical mission. Accordingly, he has this element of messianism—he wants to fulfill this mission, and he is successfully used in this.

> [Зеленского в данном случае просто используют вслепую. Ему очень удачно его окружение внушило, что он войдет в историю как великий реформатор—чуть ли не как царь Александр Второй освободитель, который отменил крепостное право… То есть, его убедили. Соответственно, у него есть вот этот элемент мессианства—он хочет эту миссию выполнить, и его удачно используют].

> (Kushch, 2021, 7:33–8:40)

Indeed, after the parliamentary meeting at which the new Land Code was adopted (it was dubbed "Walpurgis Night" because the deputies voted in masks), Zelensky (2019) posted a video in which he says that serfdom is over, and this is a historic event. Kushch's observation regarding Zelensky's belief in his progressive historical mission is in line with the basic argument of this book regarding the progressive historical imaginary behind every stage of Ukraine's neoliberalization since the collapse of the USSR.

When Zelensky dismissed Honcharuk's Cabinet in March 2020,[8] he acknowledged the external influence on sovereign Ukrainian matters by arguing that the Cabinet had "become overly solicitous of Western nations that financially support Ukraine by appointing foreigners to the boards of state companies" (Kramer, 2020). Zelensky's remark, however, did not put an end to the system in which decisive roles on the supervisory boards of state enterprises are given to foreigners. Among them are individuals such as Jost Lyngman—Permanent Representative of the International Monetary Fund in Ukraine, a citizen of the Kingdom of Sweden; Matteo Patrone—Managing Director of the European Bank for Reconstruction and Development in Eastern Europe, an Italian citizen; Jason Pellmar—the head of the regional office of the International Finance Corporation (IFC) in Ukraine and Belarus, a US citizen; and Marcin Święcicki—a Polish politician, formerly his country's Minister of Foreign Economic Relations and Deputy Minister of Economy, who has been the Business Ombudsman[9] in Ukraine since 2019 (Gubrienko, 2020). It is noteworthy that the globalists receive local remuneration. Although the question of foreigners receiving exorbitant wages for serving on advisory boards has been considered by both the Ukrainian parliament and the Supreme Court, nothing has changed.

Moreover, foreign control of Ukrainian affairs has not been limited to the appointment of so-called "sorosyata"[10] to governmental or managerial positions at state companies. If one looks at the tweets of G-7 ambassadors to Ukraine, the extent of this control becomes evident. Here are just a couple of examples of such tweets published in May 2020—the month following Honcharuk's resignation:

> During a meeting with Rada Chairman Dmytro Razumkov, the G7 Ambassadors noted the importance of securing a new IMF program and of continuing to move forward on legislation in support of reforms that will strengthen Ukraine's economy and democracy.
>
> G7AmbReformUA, 2020a)

> During a meeting with the supervisory boards of the state-owned banks and the Ministry of Finance, the G7 Ambassadors recognized the role these independent boards have played in strengthening Ukraine's financial system... In particular, they emphasized the importance of continuing reforms to improve corporate governance.
>
> (G7AmbReformUA, 2020b)

Such "encouraging" tweets are published regularly. What is easily discernable in them are the subject-position of the powerful Western states as represented by the G-7 Ambassadors, who "underscore" and "emphasize"—give instructions, in other words—and the object-position of Ukraine, which, according to the logic of the tweets, is supposed to accept these instructions and obey them without question.

The topic of Ukraine falling under the control of the global institutional regime of safeguarding the free market is inexhaustible, given that such influence is carried out in many different ways—from grants that allow "servants" of globalism to be educated in Western universities to the lobbying groups of global corporations that help to shape governmental decisions. If all the factors of this influence were accounted for, the "global institutional regime" would look like a spider's web in which Ukraine is entangled. However, what is important to acknowledge with respect to the topic of this book is that Ukraine's entanglement in the global neoliberal web has not been exclusively a matter of foreigners with evil intentions.

The entrapping looks quite logical given Ukraine's proclaimed goal of Europeanization/Westernization/neoliberalization presented as a "no alternative" developmental pathway. Ukraine has been transformed into a passive object of globalists' neoliberal mission by the internal logic of its own discourse of unidirectional progress, as its own progressive imaginary sees development exclusively in the unidirectional terms of Westernization. Acting as Edward Said's (2003) "willing intellectuals" who always have "calming words about benign and altruistic empires, as if one shouldn't trust the evidence of one's eyes watching the destruction and the misery and death brought by the latest mission civilizatrice" (p. xxi), Ukrainian "servants" of globalism have been doing their best to diminish Ukraine's sovereignty and democracy for the sake of neoliberalization. From their perspective, there has been nothing wrong with this—on the contrary, it has been seen as a course of action taken for the good of Ukraine, in line with David Harvey's (2005) observation that:

> Even the most draconian of IMF restructuring programmes is unlikely to go forward without a modicum of internal support from someone. It sometimes seems as if the IMF merely takes the responsibility for doing what some internal class forces want to do anyway.
>
> (117)

But in Ukraine's case, the "internal class" which Harvey mentions is not entirely "internal"—many advocates of Ukraine's neoliberalization have been educated abroad and are closely connected with global neoliberal institutions. In this sense, they represent not an internal class so much as an international one—a class of globalists whose unity has been forged by the discourse of unidirectional progress which places the West in the leading role. As outlined in Chapter 1, all of the neoliberal reformers of post-Soviet Ukraine have been employing this discourse, and in this sense Zelensky is not an exception.

What distinguishes Zelensky among post-Soviet neoliberals and makes his case exceptional is his populism forged on the fringes of the virtual and the real. Founded on the rigid juxtaposition of "the good people" and "the corrupted elites," Zelensky's populism has turned out to be very handy for the further incorporation of Ukraine into the global neoliberal project. If all local politicians are stupid and corrupt, it is only natural to ask for foreign advice and accept guidance from beyond the nation's borders. Both the logic of his unidirectional progressive imaginary and Zelensky's Manichean division of the social into an irreconcilable dichotomy have created a fertile soil for this dependency to flourish. As a result, the democratic energy of the Ukrainian people, which made Zelensky's progressive-neoliberal machine a success, has been exploited to ensure that this energy would be contained and that democracy would still be "to come" (Derrida, 2002, p. 105)—a perpetual promise throughout all of Ukraine's post-Soviet transformations.

Notes

1 The Orange Revolution began on the eve of the second round of the presidential election of 2004, when the official count differed substantially from the results of exit polling that gave Victor Yushchenko—an oppositional candidate—up to an 11 percent lead. The official results gave the election win to Victor Yanukovych—the protégé of then incumbent President Leonid Kuchma—by 3 percent. Huge protests against what was seen by the protesters as "massive fraud" resulted in Yushchenko's victory.

2 As Minister of Finance of Ukraine, Jaresko implemented "the largest IMF program in the institution's history" (FOMB, n/d). After her tenure in Ukraine, she was designated Executive Director of the Financial Oversight and Management Board for Puerto Rico.

3 As a minister, Abromavičius advocated for deregulation, privatization, austerity, and a reduced role for the state in economic processes (Brian & Verstyuk, 2014). After leaving his ministerial position, he was appointed Director General of Ukroboronprom, Ukraine's biggest defense industry company (2019–2020).

4 Before coming to Ukraine, Kvitashvili was Minister of Health of Georgia (2008–2010). During his ministerial tenure in Ukraine, Kvitashvili was wanted by the Georgian government—he had been accused of destroying the Georgian healthcare system (Civil Georgia, December 20, 2014).

5 Suprun's healthcare reform, provided under the slogan "money follows the patient," presupposed shutting down ineffective clinics with a small number of patients. Opposition called this monetized healthcare policy "genocide of the Ukrainian people"; Suprun was nicknamed "Dr. Death" (Pimm, 2018).

6 Oksana Markarova holds a master's degree in international public finance and trade from the University of Indiana (USA). Before assuming her governmental position, she worked as an economic policy advisor and manager for external and corporate communications at Western NIS Enterprise Fund, a US direct investment fund, and as head of the board (President) of ITT-Invest company. Markarova was also an intern at the World Bank, where she worked in the group in charge of the banking sector and financial markets in Europe and Middle Asia (Markarova, n/d).

7 Tymofiy Mylovanov, PhD, got his doctoral degree in economics at the University of Wisconsin–Madison (USA). During his professional career, he has been teaching at European and American universities including Rheinische Friedrich–Wilhelms–Universität Bonn, the University of Pennsylvania, and the University of Pittsburgh. Before assuming his governmental position, Mylovanov was elected to the board of the National Bank of Ukraine and served as the board's deputy chairman from 2016 to 2019 (Mylovanov, n/d).

8 After his resignation, Honcharuk became a distinguished fellow of the Atlantic Council—a think tank whose website, in keeping with the core principles of neoliberal thought, states that "market economies underpinned by the rule of law and stable democratic systems generate prosperity for their citizens, drive innovation, and create global opportunities for growth" (Atlantic Council, n/d). What distinguished Honcharuk, according to the Council's website, was precisely his merit in the field of Ukraine's neoliberalization— among other things, the site states, Honcharuk "initiated the adoption [of] legislation that aided the introduction of land reform; commenced the implementation of medical and educational reforms… [and]… launched wide privatization processes" (Atlantic Council, n/d). Needless to say, the bond affair was not listed among Honcharuk's achievements.

9 The mission of the Business Ombudsman Council is to provide "greater transparency of business practices in Ukraine" (Business Ombudsma Counciln, n/d).

10 The term "sorosyata"—a popular meme in Ukrainian political discourse— is derived from the surname of the famous American billionaire investor George Soros. "Sorosyata" are widely believed to represent the interests of global neoliberal institutions or simply the West as a whole (Demyachuk, 2021).

References

Atlantic Council. (n/d). Oleksiy Honcharuk. Retrieved from https://www.atlanticcouncil.org/expert/oleksiy-honcharuk

Babb, S. (2009). *Behind the development banks.* Chicago, IL: University of Chicago Press.

Bonefeld, W. (2015). European economic constitution and the transformation of democracy: On class and the state of law. *European Journal of International Relations, 21*(4), 867–886. doi: 10.1177/1354066115570158

Brian, B., & Verstyuk, I. (2014, December 15). New economy minister stands for austerity. Kyiv Post. Retrieved from https://www.kyivpost.com/article/content/reform-watch/new-economy-minister-stands-for-austerity-deregulation-privatization-375191.html

Brown, W. (2018, January 18). Who is not a neoliberal today? *Tocqueville 21.* Retrieved from www.tocqueville21.com/interviews/wendy-brown-not-neoliberal-today

Business Ombudsman Council. (n/d). About. Retrieved from https://boi.org.ua/en/about/

Chorev, N. (2005). The institutional project of neo-liberal globalism: The case of the WTO. *Theory and Society, 34*(3), 317–355. doi: 10.1007/s11186-005-6301-9

Civil Georgia. (2014, December 20). Garibashvili says ex-Georgian officials in Ukrainian govt 'damaging' ties. Retrieved from https://old.civil.ge/eng/article.php?id=27926

Delo.ua. (2020, January 15). У Зеленского примитивное понимание экономических процессов [Zelensky has a primitive understanding of economic processes]. Retrieved from https://delo.ua/econonomyandpolitic-sinukraine/u-zelenskogo-primitivnoe-ponimanie-ekonomicheski-363371/

Demyachuk, T. (2021, January 25). "Sorosyata" and "external governance" of Ukraine: A conspiracy narrative fueling anti-Western discourse. *European Security Journal.* Retrieved from https://www.esjnews.com/sorosyata-and-external-governance-of-ukraine-a-conspiracy-narrative-fuelling-anti-western-discourse

Derrida, J. (2002). *Who's afraid of philosophy: Right to philosophy.* Stanford, CA: Stanford University Press.

Farrant, A., McPhail, E., & Berger, S. (2012). Preventing the "abuses" of democracy: Hayek, the "military usurper" and transitional dictatorship in Chile? *American Journal of Economics and Sociology, 71*(3), 513–538. doi: 10.1111/j.1536–7150.2012.00824.x

FOMB. (n/d). Natalie Jaresko: Executive director & interim revitalization coordinator. *Financial Oversight and Management Board for Puerto Rico.* Retrieved from https://oversightboard.pr.gov/natalie-jaresko/

G7AmbReformUA. (2020a, May 7). During a meeting with Rada Chairman… *Twitter.* Retrieved from https://twitter.com/G7AmbReformUA/status/1258412078316093441

G7AmbReformUA. (2020b, May 22). During a meeting with the supervisory boards… Twitter. Retrieved from https://twitter.com/G7AmbReformUA/status/1263818725553250305/photo/1

Gubrienko, R. (2020, August 30). Наблюдательные советы в госкомпаниях: иностранный контроль за счет бюджета [Supervisory Boards in State-owned Companies: Foreign budget control]. *Vesti.ua.* Retrieved from https://vesti.ua/politika/nablyudatelnye-sovety-v-goskompaniyah-inostrannyj-kontrol-za-schet-byudzheta

Harmes, A. (2006). Neoliberalism and multilevel governance. *Review of International Political Economy, 13*(5): 725–749. doi: 10.1080/09692290600950621

Harvey, D. (2005). *A brief history of neoliberalism.* Oxford, MA: Oxford University Press.

Kozak, M. (2020, April 24). Will the bond flood the Ukrainian economy? *Obserwator Finansowy.* Retrieved from https://www.obserwatorfinansowy.pl/in-english/will-the-bond-flood-the-ukrainian-economy

Kramer, A. E. (2020, March 4). Ukraine's Zelensky fires his cabinet. *New York Times.* Retrieved from https://www.nytimes.com/2020/03/04/world/europe/ukraine-zelensky-cabinet.html

Kushch, A. (2021, June 10). Рынок земли—одна из самых больших ошибок нынешней власти [The land market is one of the biggest mistakes of the current government]. YouTube. Retrieved from https://www.youtube.com/watch?v=YTOs7ThtLFo

Markarova, O. (n/d). Ambassador Extraordinary and Plenipotentiary of Ukraine to the United States. Ambassy of Ukraine in the USA. Retrieved from https://usa.mfa.gov.ua/en/gov ernance/oksana-markarova

Mylovanov, T. (n/d). KSE President, Associate Professor of the University of Pittsburgh. Kyiv School of Economics. Retrieved from https://kse.ua/people/tymofiy-mylovanov

Pimm, J. (2018). Ulana Suprun: the accidental reformer. *The Lancet, 392*(10149), 727.

Polanyi, K. (2001). *The great transformation: The political and economic origins of our time*. Boston, MA: Beacon Press.

Said, E. W. (2003). *Orientalism*. New York: Pantheon Books.

Slobodian, Q. (2020). *Globalists: The end of empire and the birth of neoliberalism*. Cambridge, MA: Harvard University Press.

Tyshchuk, O. (2017, August 9). 12 иностранцев, которые приехали реформировать Украину [12 foreigners who came to reform Ukraine]. *Fakty*. Retrieved from https://fakty.com.ua/ru/ukraine/20170809-12-inozemtsiv-yaki-pryyihaly-reformuvaty-ukrayinu

Vishnevsky, Y. (2020, February 13). Десять соросят [Ten sorosyats]. *DS News*. Retrieved from https://www.dsnews.ua/politics/desyat-sorosyat-kto-iz-lyudey-sorosa-stal-samym-vliyatelnym-12022020220000

Yurchenko, Y. (2018). *Ukraine and the empire of capital: From marketization to armed conflict*. London: Pluto Press.

Zelensky, V. (2019, November 13). Рабства больше не будет! [There will be no more slavery!]. YouTube. Retrieved from https://www.youtube.com/watch?v=KD6T61vDrNs

Conclusion

The story of Zelensky's ascent to power and realizing of unpopular neoliberal reforms consists of several parts, each of which provides serious grounds to reflect on established modes of thinking about contemporary political communication. To start with, Zelensky's show served as a virtual election platform, with the comedian explaining to Ukrainians through his performances as President Holoborodko what should be done to modernize Ukraine so that it could make "civilizational" progress. Using a TV show as an informal political platform is an unusual development. It suggests that scholars of communication should not restrict themselves to the scholarly hegemonic framework when analyzing contemporary political processes. We should not limit ourselves by analyzing only conventional election platforms, official speeches and interviews, media coverage of election campaigns, social media exchanges, and so forth. Attention should be paid to new, unconventional forms of political communication, where "political" is understood in broad terms of contesting and negotiating meanings (Laclau & Mouffe, 1985)—an incessant process permeating all aspects of collective life within our highly stratified and digitalized societies. If meanings are contested, negotiated, and hegemonized in both real and virtual realms; if they are constructed both verbally and performatively; if the borders between politics and entertainment blur; then all the complexity of discursive-material assemblages should be accounted for—the hybridization of the imagined and the real, the artistic and the political, the digital and the tangible, and so forth.

In this respect, it is important to underline that in spite of all its originality, Zelensky's case has one obvious aspect in which it is not unique: In our highly digitalized social environment, almost all political promises are made "virtually." George W. Bush's "Windsurfing" (2004), Barack Obama's "Yes We Can" (2008), Donald Trump's "Argument for America" (2016), and all other political ads get their

DOI: 10.4324/9781003228493-10

viewers through the materiality of the interface ostensibly separating "the virtual" and "the real." Not only conventional political ads, but ads of any kind—whether nonprofit or commercial—are produced and distributed digitally these days, with a major question being to what extent they "reproduce" analogue "reality" and to what extent they create it by acting as power agents of their own. Zelensky has gone further than others—mixing together the virtual, the real, the political, and the artistic in ways that leave little chance to differentiate between them—but this does not negate the fact that hybrids of all sorts inhabit contemporary societies, communicating with each other across established boundaries and breaking them down. This reminds us of the necessity to update conventional analytical tools that can no longer make sense of the complexity of such boundless communication processes. New analytical perspectives are needed, and this book has offered just one of them—Carpentier's (2017) Discursive-Material Knot enriched with the dimension of digital materiality.

Connecting the virtual and the real through recognizing the materiality of the former makes analysis richer. But this is not only about richness or simply "doing justice to the agential material," as Carpentier (2021, p. 112) claims; this is also a matter of comprehension. In the highly digitalized contemporary world, it is simply impossible to separate the digital/intangible/virtual into an autonomous realm ostensibly differentiated from the "real" world, as scholars working in digital discourse studies readily acknowledge. Increasingly, such scholars have been challenging the distinction between the offline/real/tangible and the online/virtual/intangible as well as highlighting the impact of multi-modality on the production of meanings (e.g., Bolander & Locher, 2020). As their research suggests, most Internet users do not see the online and offline spheres of their activities as distinct; rather, the online is seen as an extension of the offline—a prolongation of the social.

Second, Zelensky's unprecedented electoral success, forged on the fringes of the virtual and the real, enabled him to create a parliamentary machine capable of rubber-stamping laws for neoliberal reform under the guidance of global neoliberal institutions and their agents, without regard for Ukraine's political opposition or public opinion. A lesson we can draw from this is that Hayek's ideas still endure and prevail, despite the widely shared belief about "the old" that "is dying" (Fraser, 2019). As early as 1944, in his historic work *The Road to Serfdom*, Hayek wrote:

> Free trade and freedom of opportunity are ideas which still may arouse the imagination of large numbers, but a mere 'reasonable

freedom of trade' or a mere 'relaxation of controls' is neither intellectually respectable nor likely to inspire any enthusiasm. The main lesson which the true liberal must learn from the success of the socialists is that it was their *courage to be Utopian* which gained them the support of the intellectuals and therefore an influence on public opinion which is daily making possible what only recently seemed utterly remote.

(2013, p. 129, emphasis added)

As Zelensky's case demonstrates, Hayek's disciples took his recommendation seriously. It was the utopia of an ideal Ukrainian society, created by Zelensky on his show, that made possible "what only recently seemed utterly remote": using a local comedian to entrench global neoliberalism, utilizing a fictional TV series to dislocate the normality of the hegemonic political discourse, operating a virtual-real party machine to control the excesses of democracy, etc. The lesson we should learn from this part of Zelensky's story is that one should not forget about capitalism's "incredible resilience... its remarkable capacity to survive its own periodic crises and find new spatial and technological fixes," as Lara Monticelli (2018, p. 503) put it.

In this respect, the value of Fraser's (2019) observation that, to gain broader appeal, neoliberalism needs to repackage itself—to deck itself out as progressive—is hard to overestimate. To be successful, Zelensky's neoliberal project had to be euphemized through articulating links not with mass privatization, budget cuts, land sales, and so forth, but with civil peace, social justice, Europeanization, and modernization—in other words, "progress." A remarkable capacity to adapt was demonstrated by switching links between the primary signifiers of the progressive discourse when it was tactically necessary. As outlined in Chapter 3, during the pre-election period, while acting as Holoborodko, Zelensky equivalentially linked "modernization" with anti-corruption efforts, de-oligarchization, and social justice (de-privatization of collective property and redistribution of public wealth); in the post-election period (2019–2020), while acting as the real president of Ukraine, Zelensky connected "modernization" with neoliberal reforms: privatization of public property, reducing the power of trade unions, making labor laws more flexible, and so forth. Later, amid a collapsing approval rating, Zelensky "returned" to promises he had made to Ukrainians as the fictional Holoborodko, pursuing de-oligarchization and re-privatization in a bid to revive his popularity. This is a good illustration of how, to survive, a neoliberal project can "change its skin" back and forth.

Accordingly, it is worthy highlighting that as a tool for selling a neoliberal pig in a populist poke, humor came to be indispensable. A passage from Slavoj Žižek (2018) about Donald Trump can easily be applied to Zelensky in this regard:

> The problem is not that Trump is a clown. The problem is that there is a programme behind his provocations, a method in his madness… [that is]… part of their populist strategy to sell this programme to ordinary people, a programme which (in the long term, at least) works against ordinary people: lower taxes for the rich, less healthcare and workers' protection, etc. Unfortunately, people are ready to swallow many things if they are presented to them through laughter.

This is exactly what we observe in the case of Zelensky. Making fun of the "exploiters" of the Ukrainian people—placing these powerful figures in an object-position—created a cathartic moment of enjoyment shared by Zelensky's viewers. It is this moment of enjoyment that was exploited by Zelensky to create a broad populist front of Ukrainians against the nation's "parasites."

Finally, we should not lose sight of the fact that Zelensky's project, amid all its artistic originality, drew its strength from unprecedented popular support. It is important to recognize that Ukrainians liked Zelensky's program of authoritarian "normalization" as presented on his show: the imprisonment of oligarchs and the confiscation of their property with no trial; the firing of officials without any hearings in court; the blackmailing, threatening, and intimidating of corrupted politicians, and so on. By supporting this virtual program, Ukrainians seemed to be reveling in the possibility of such autocratic governance, which Zelensky started to implement in reality in early 2021 as he attempted to salvage his popularity. Cannot we interpret this as a sign of popular fatigue with the discourse of rule of law and democracy, under the guise of which all post-Soviet neoliberal experiments were set into motion? Is this not an indication of people's secret awareness that under the rule of the market, the notion of equality for all before the law is an illusion? Cannot this be interpreted as the people's reaction to a neoliberal onslaught against the common good, which they have been experiencing since the advent of post-Soviet neoliberal times? Is this not a reaction to the market forces that, since being unleashed, have damaged society by eroding people's belief in justice (Brown, 2019)? These questions—only reformulated with respect to the specifics of other societies—require more scholarly attention as support among electorates for populists who euphemize their neoliberal agendas by wrapping them in enticing covers is a significant factor contributing to neoliberalism's incredible ability to survive.

Discussing this issue in the context of the "deepening divisions, even hatred" existing between Trump supporters and progressives, Fraser argues that a substantial part of the misunderstanding between the former and the latter is due to "reactionary impulses" stemming "from a *ressentiment* against progressive-neoliberal moralizing" (Fraser & Jaeggi, 2018, p. 219, emphasis original). Fraser's observations regarding U.S. progressives who are confident "that they represent the advance guard of humanity's progression to moral cosmopolitanism and cognitive enlightenment" (Fraser & Jaeggi, 2018, p. 208) are in line with my own findings from Russia and Ukraine. Analyzing the emancipatory rhetoric of local social movements, I found that their activists habitually diminished and marginalized their presumably "underdeveloped" and "unenlightened" compatriots, and excluded their voices from deliberation on important issues within "progressive" public spheres (Baysha, 2018). If this is a global trend, then we need to open our minds not only to suppressed possibilities for development—a typical aim within the exercise of critical thinking—but also to those "deplorables" (Hillary Clinton's expression) whom we seem to be intellectually unequipped to understand.

As a result of this inability to see another perspective, "progressives"— who have "devolved all too easily into moralizing, finger-pointing, and talking down to rural and working-class people, with the insinuation that they were culturally backward or stupid" (Fraser & Jaeggi, 2018, p. 208)—draw solid dividing frontiers between themselves and "retrograde" forces, deepening existing antagonisms and giving rise to new ones. By fostering these divisions through unproductive moralizing, social activists and critical scholars may inadvertently contribute to the entrenchment of global neoliberalism.

To end the prolonged era of global neoliberal governance, those striving for social justice, understood in democratic terms of social equality, need to equip themselves intellectually so that we might finally begin to avoid homogenization, hierarchization, essentialization, and moralization—all the aspects of antagonistic discourse (Carpentier, 2017) that the term "deplorables" and its synonyms ("sovki," "vatniki," "serfs," etc.) embody. As Fraser put it, "That these movements focus their ire on immigrants does not prove the overwhelming majority of their supporters are incorrigible racists, although some of them undoubtedly are" (Fraser & Jaeggi, 2018, p. 197). In a similar fashion, we can argue: "That the admirers of Holoborodko supported his authoritarian

methods of government does not prove that none of them value legality, equality, and social justice, although some of them do not." In
other words, we need to be able to see the internal diversity of "cultural
others"—to make porous the apparently solid and impermeable barriers
between the self and our potential allies. This will allow the activation
of a diversity of positions, the forging of connections between former
"enemies," and the creation of alliances across borders. Without the
development of such anti-neoliberal alliances, neoliberalism will hardly
die, despite all the popular discontentment it engenders. Rather, it may
reappear again and again in different guises around the world. This is
the main lesson to be learned from the story of Zelensky-Holoborodko.

References

Baysha, O. (2018). *Miscommunicating social change: Lessons from Russia and Ukraine*. Lanham, MD: Lexington.

Bolander, B., & Locher, M. A. (2020). Beyond the online offline distinction: Entry points to digital discourse. *Discourse, Context & Media, 35*, 1–9. doi: 10.1016/j.dcm.2020.100383

Brown, W. (2019). *In the ruins of neoliberalism*. New York: Columbia University Press.

Carpentier, N. (2017). *The discursive-material knot: Cyprus in conflict and community media participation*. New York: Peter Lang.

Carpentier, N. (2021). Doing justice to the agential material: A reflection on a non-hierarchical repositioning of the discursive and the material. *Journal of Language and Politics, 20*(1), 112–128. doi: 10.1075/jlp.20045.car

Fraser, N. (2019). *The old is dying and the new cannot be born: From progressive neoliberalism to Trump and Beyond*. New York: Verso.

Fraser, N., & Jaeggi, R. (2018). *Capitalism: A conversation in critical theory*. New York: John Wiley & Sons.

Hayek, F. A. (2013). *The road to serfdom*. London: Institute of Economic Affairs.

Laclau, E., & Mouffe, C. (1985). *Hegemony and socialist strategy: Towards a radical democratic politics*. London: Verso.

Monticelli, L. (2018). Embodying alternatives to capitalism in the 21st century. *TripleC, 16*(2), 501–517. doi: 10.31269/triplec.v16i2.1032

Žižek, S. (2018). The prospects of radical change today. *TripleC, 16*(2), 476–489. doi: 10.31269/triplec.v16i2.1023

Index